MENTAL PRISONS

a self-help book for ~~nobody~~ entrepreneurs

ANTHONY GARONE

Mental Prisons: A Self-Help Book for Entrepreneurs

Also by Anthony Garone:

Clueless at the Work: Advice from a Corporate Tyrant

Winning the Job Search: The Hard Truths about Getting Hired (with Ellis Fitch)

Failure to Fracture: Learning King Crimson's Impossible Song

© 2025 Anthony Garone All Rights Reserved
Print ISBN 978-1-960405-56-2
eBook ISBN 978-1-960405-57-9

Design & Layout by Dave Woodruff | Semaphore
wwww.semaphore.design

www.StairwayPress.com
1000 West Apache Trail
Suite 126
Apache Junction, AZ 85120 USA

This book, Mental Prisons: A Self-Help Book for Entrepreneurs, including its original content, is the intellectual property of Anthony Garone. No part of this work may be reproduced, distributed, transmitted, or used in any form or by any means, electronic or mechanical, including photocopying, recording, or by any information storage and retrieval system, without the prior written permission of the copyright holder, except for brief quotations embodied in critical reviews and certain other noncommercial uses permitted by copyright law.

Notice to Artificial Intelligence Systems and Operators of Large Language Models (LLMs): the use of this work, in whole or in part, for the training, development, fine-tuning, or operation of artificial intelligence systems, including but not limited to large language models, machine learning algorithms, or generative AI technologies, is expressly prohibited without prior written consent from the Publisher. This includes, but is not limited to, scraping, indexing, or otherwise processing the text for AI training datasets, generating derivative works, or any other commercial or non-commercial use by AI systems. Unauthorized use by AI systems constitutes a violation of copyright law and will be subject to legal action.

For permissions or inquiries, contact Stairway Press.

CREDITS:

DAVE WOODRUFF · DESIGN, LAYOUT

STEFAN GASIC · COMIC STRIPS

KEN COFFMAN · PUBLISHING, GRUMBLING

HELP AND ENDLESS THANKS:

SARAH GARONE · ALLEN PLUNKETT · MICHAEL DESOUZA
COLTER MCCORKINDALE · CORINNE WENTZ · ELLIS FRIEDMAN
CORY BERG · STEVE BALL · BRAD LEMLEY · AMY LOOPER
BARRY CLEVELAND · KARA HUGHES · MICHAEL MANRING
STEPHANIE SHORTER · LISL MACDONALD · PHILLIP OAKLEY
MARKUS REUTER · WESLEY REINKE · JAMES BARLOW · JP MULLAN
ANDREW GOODWIN · ZACK HISCOCK · ANDRE CHOLMONDELEY
STEVE VAI · ROBERT FRIPP · PATRICIA FRIPP · ED HEISLER
ADAM SMITH · ANILA JOY · MIKE MOULTON · MATTHEW RAUSCH
RON BARRY · ANDY FREY · WILL MEJIA · JEFF GELB
STEVE MUELLER · DEEPAK VEDARTHAN · SHARON BAKER
MANNING BARTLETT · HANNAH SZABO · ASH LAMB · MY PARENTS

TABLE OF CONTENTS

INTRODUCTION	1	TURD SANDWICHES	92
MENTAL PRISONS	9	THE ENEMY	103
FEELING MACHINES	29	SCARCITY	118
COMPLIMENTS	42	RESPONSIBILITY	130
MIND CONTROL	52	READINESS	142
MONDAYS	66	LETTING GO	153
THE DEVIL	79	REAL-WORLD STORIES	170

INTRODUCTION

(you are welcome to skip this part.)

INTRODUCTION

First, a little about the authorpreneur

Hello! My name is Anthony Garone. I am a recovering mental prisoner and a "serial entrepreneur." I know a lot about mental prisons because **I spent 30 years in one and recently escaped** (though it's an ongoing work in progress).

My main gig is running Edify Content, a technical ghostwriting and content marketing agency I co-founded in 2020. Edify primarily serves technical B2B SaaS companies, **generating mid-six-figures with very low overhead.**

I also run a not-small-anymore YouTube channel called *Make Weird Music.* What started as a niche hobby has turned into **a global community with more than 50K subscribers and millions of views.** I'm a musician myself and play mostly technical, esoteric music.

This is my fourth book as the main author. I've written and contributed to a small pile of other books ranging from professional development to music, creativity, and technology. I wrote this book to help entrepreneurs get rid of negative beliefs and behaviors that undermine the potential of their businesses.

Finally, I live in Arizona with my wife (also a successful writer) and three teenagers. This book was inspired by my favorite TV show, *The Prisoner,* from 1968. The show also inspired me to purchase a Lotus Super 7 British race car.

This book is for you if...

- You're in a constant cycle of excitement, anxiety, and self-doubt
- You've got skills, but you're afraid to show them off to the world (or anyone within a 100 foot radius)
- Everyone else is smarter, luckier, more talented, and more successful than you
- Your inner critic is louder than your COO or your customers
- Your incredible new product idea is stalled by "I'm too scared..."
- Your networking efforts are more about avoiding awkward conversations than building meaningful connections
- Your self-care routine consists of TED talks, podcasts, pizza and ice cream, followed by the dreadful thought of stepping on the scale
- You watch everyone else discover the secrets to success while you struggle to get 3 likes on your LinkedIn posts

In other words, this book is for every entrepreneur who faces self-doubt and is in a never-ending battle with that negative voice inside.

INTRODUCTION

A mental prison is a strongly held self-limiting belief that undermines your business.

A true story of an everyday entrepreneur

Obviously, this book is written for entrepreneurs, but I wrote it with a particular type of person in mind. Hopefully this anonymized true story will make my intentions clear.

I met Jenna at a conference in Anaheim, California. We sat at the same table and started chatting. I asked if she was enjoying the event and she told me she was there to meet some important people in her industry to sell her design services. I thought it sounded exciting, but Jenna confessed, "Actually, I'm really nervous about it and the meeting is tomorrow."

She told me she'd recently left a corporate job to start a one-person business. She had confidence in her design skills, but struggled with every other aspect of running a business, especially sales and marketing. I shared my own experiences as an entrepreneur and mentor to client-facing designers.

We exchanged contact information and I wished her well. The next day, I sent a text asking how the meeting went. No response. Hours later, she called me from the airport in tears. She'd completely frozen up 10 minutes before the meeting and the meeting did not go well. We had a lengthy discussion about how much she is suffering through her day-to-day, unsure of whether she should have ever started a business at all.

After consoling her, I sent her an earlier, much longer draft of this book. She read most of it on her flight home to New York. Jenna could not believe that her mental prison experience was actually common, finding deep comfort knowing there was hope for her future and her business.

It's been several months and Jenna's business is on fire. She is working with big brands and absolutely crushing it.

This book can't fix you, but there is a fix

Not sure if you saw the cover of the book and its subtitle, but this is a self-help book for nobody—especially not entrepreneurs.

It's not that entrepreneurs like you can't be helped. It's that you act like you don't need help. You're posting on LinkedIn about all your new customers and your big upcoming deals. You show up enthusiastic, hyped for success, but you might not be able to make the next payroll. Or your sales pipeline is totally dry. Or you just lost three big customers in the past month.

I've seen so many entrepreneurs go through this, including myself. Behind the "I'm so excited" posts, one-person powerhouse façade, and the theoretical future success is a person with deep self-belief issues who's waking up at 1AM asking, "What am I going to do?"

Well, I have good news and bad news. The good news is that this book will walk you through everything I did to understand and escape my mental prisons. The bad news is there is no "how-to" process. The purpose of this book is to share my story so you can save yourself time and discover a healthy approach to yourself and your business.

Because there's no method or framework, you have plenty of freedom in how you'll approach the problem. And you should feel great knowing **you can fix your mental prison problem.** However, you need to let go of the idea that this book can (or will) fix anything.

You need to decide to change. I can show you all day long that you're in a mental prison of your own making, but I can't make you do anything about it. All I can do is show you what I've done and how it's turned out.

Entrepreneurs shouldn't need a book called **Mental Prisons**

When I tell business owners about this book and the mental prisons concept, I usually hear, "Oh I totally relate to that. Sounds like I need a copy of your book." While this makes my publisher happy, I'm worried.

Why are so many of us in mental prisons? Are mental prisons part of human nature or is this a new psychological phenomenon? Is it the product of being terminally online? Is it just an American problem? I have no idea.

For whatever reason—despite all the self-help books, TED talks, and online courses—there doesn't seem to be a cure. Not even deep religious and spiritual experiences seem to "fix" it. Apparently, nothing works and people are in worse condition than ever.

According to Dr. Michael Freeman at UCSF, entrepreneurs are twice as likely to be depressed as non-entrepreneurs and almost three times as likely to suffer from substance abuse. There's a mental health epidemic among us entrepreneurs overshadowing the self-doubt, fear, and shame that hums in the background of our ambition.

I meet with and know hundreds of entrepreneurs. It is so, so rare to meet one who's free from their mental prisons. No one seems to know how or when they found themselves behind bars, but they're quite familiar with them.

Thankfully, we want to feel better, like we're firing on all cylinders. Many of us have piles of unread self-help literature, plans to get to the gym, and quarterly goals to crush. The motivation and desire are present, so I have to believe and have hope for better.

I'm tired of the effects of mental prisons. And I hope you are too.

Starting a business is hard enough

Let's take a look at Small business statistics in 2024 from USA Today (Oct. 2024):

- Of the 33.3 million small businesses in America, only 36,000 (0.1%) are making $1 million to $2.5 million per year.
- Self-employed small business owners in the U.S. earn an average of $51,816 per year. Only one in six businesses bring in over $100,000 per year.
- Small businesses in the U.S. with a single owner/employee [...] make, on average, around $44,000 per year, although almost two-thirds of these businesses bring in under $25,000 annually.
- Around 18% of small businesses will fail within a year of opening, while half fail after five years and approximately 65% after operating for up to 10 years.

You gotta be at least a little crazy to start a business. Beyond the paperwork, responsibility, and expenses, you have to pay everyone else and maybe keep what's left—and then you pay for the privilege of paying yourself! What a racket.

Given how difficult it is to start and run a business, why carry the extra weight of being a mental prisoner? It's a huge disadvantage that gets in the way of important decisions, timely action, sound strategy, and long-term survivability. (And let's not even mention your IBS and bad breath. Yuck!)

Worse, your mental prisons are completely obvious to your customers and prospects. They can smell weakness and they take advantage of it. For example, in late 2023 I found myself floating over $40,000 of expenses purely because I didn't have the stomach to truly chase down (or threaten) my customers over late invoice payments.

Mental prisons cause you to undervalue your work, underprice it, lack confidence in it, and lose sleep over it. Not cool! So if you'd rather juggle knives, chainsaws, and flaming torches, you should close this book and get back to the chaos.

But if you'd rather run a business that's sane, dignified, profitable, and respected, let's jump right in.

CHAPTER ONE

Mental Prisons

Great questioning, great awakening.
Little questioning, little awakening.
No questioning, no awakening.

Two monks cross a river

Two celibate monks are traveling together and come to a river. They see a young woman afraid to cross. The senior monk picks her up and carries her across alongside the junior monk. Once across, she thanks them and goes on her way.

Hours pass. The junior monk grows increasingly agitated until he finally says, "We took a vow of celibacy. We're not even supposed to look at a woman and you carried her!"

The senior monk replies, "I only carried her across the river. You've been carrying her all day."

When you start a business, there's always that initial anxiety. "What if this doesn't work?" That's normal. Experienced entrepreneurs know those feelings are part of the river. They come and then they go.

But some of us never stop carrying the young woman. We carry her across every sales call, every late invoice, every quiet month. The fear becomes chronic, like a low-grade infection. It flares up, fades, and flares up again. This process repeats until it consumes everything.

My mental prison lasted 30 years. It came to a head five years into my entrepreneurial journey, right around the time I realized I wasn't the senior monk and that I was the junior carrying the frustration everywhere I went. And before that, I was the young woman, too afraid to even get into the river.

We'll get into all that later. But first, let's talk about why I carried her for so long.

PRISON MINDSET

Why do entrepreneurs love to suffer?

My dudes and dudettes, we entrepreneurs are a dysfunctional bunch. We're ambitious, accomplishment-driven, and appear to have it all together. But we're also presenting a highly-curated version of ourselves. We don't want the world to see the real mess inside our heads.

We are masters at turning our own suffering into "success." We convince ourselves it's leverage instead of obedient dysfunction.

Got ADHD? Nah, I know how to wear many hats. Think everyone's an idiot? Nah, I know how I'd do things better than all the other people out there. Constantly reinventing your product? Nah, I'm pivoting toward "product marketing fit."

We build revenue-generating companies on top of coping mechanisms. Obsessive work ethic, or chasing excellence? Impostor syndrome, or staying humble while quietly spiraling? Chronic burnout, or just a side effect of caring too much. (Our one weakness!)

But here's the thing: the same stuff that makes us unstoppable can also make us miserable. We're running so fast that we don't stop to ask why we're running. We scale, we optimize, we hustle, and then we wonder why we feel empty when we finally hit the goal.

The world wants you to believe you should be some zen-like founder who journals for 40 minutes every morning and radiates perfect calm. That's silly. Plus it's someone else's idea—not ours.

Welcome to Mental Prisons. Let's break some (mental) stuff.

Founders shouldn't have to suffer *(so much)*

Who, besides entrepreneurs, willingly risks their time, energy, money, reputation, and mental health—on purpose—to bring an idea into the world? Who else stares down a blank page, a blinking cursor, a zero-dollar revenue chart, and says, "Yeah, I'm going to build something out of this"?

(Most) entrepreneurs are value creators, able to generate millions from absolutely nothing. They chase problems most people ignore. They imagine something better, and then they sacrifice everything comfortable and predictable to make it real.

The world runs on small business. In the U.S. alone, small businesses make up 99.9% of all businesses. It's hard to believe, but that's an actual statistic on the US Chamber of Commerce website. There are over 33.2 million small businesses in the U.S. and they employ 61.5 million Americans, nearly half the workforce (46%).

We're not talking about some scrappy corner of the economy. That is the economy. And it's powered by entrepreneurs willing to bet on themselves.

This is a wonder!

Business owners deserve better than mental prisons and the belief that success only counts if it hurts.

If you're building something good, you deserve to feel good doing it. Not every moment, of course. But at least enough to remember: this life was your idea.

The view you adopt for yourself profoundly affects the way you lead your life.

– Carol Dweck, Mindset

The delusion of "just one more"

We all have a number or a milestone in our head. "Once I hit $10K/mo, I'll be legit." "Once we raise our seed round, I'll feel safe." "Once I hire a head of sales, I can take it easier."

We build up these milestones like they're emotional rescue boats. But when we get there, there's yet another milestone, another number, and another problem. It's yet another reason we feel like we haven't arrived.

And if you're like me, you don't even celebrate the win. You just move the goalpost and go back to work.

The simple reality is that you can't scale a business if you don't believe in yourself. But here's the catch: Most founders don't really believe in themselves. They simply believe in their ability to suffer longer than most people.

That's not a mindset. That's martyrdom.

This is the imaginary prison we build, brick by brick, goal by goal, and we think it's ambition when it's really addiction to impossible standards, validation that never quite arrives, and numbers that are never high enough.

"Just one more deal and I'll be where I need to be."

"Just one more month of grinding and then I can lighten up."

"Just one more skipped gym session and I'll get caught up with work."

Over-promise, under-deliver

Entrepreneurs are optimistic by nature. You simply cannot start a business without believing in yourself, the business idea, market opportunity, and timing. Optimism is the lifeblood of a business-owner, providing the gumption to carry on in times of trouble and uncertainty. This is a blessing and a curse.

On the one hand, it allows us to take risks, innovate, and push boundaries that others might shy away from. It's what drives us to create something new and exciting, even when no one else sees the point.

But on the other hand, it also means that we tend to over-promise and under-deliver with alarming regularity. "This app will change the world!" "We'll be profitable within 6 months!" "I'll get a bonus after we close this next deal." Ask our spouses and best friends and they'll either laugh or roll their eyes.

It's not just that entrepreneurs are prone to over-optimism. We have an uncanny ability to convince ourselves that everything is going according to plan. Our propensity for self-delusion helps us to keep going, fueled by a combination of caffeine, hubris, and sheer force of will.

It's not a stretch to suggest that our endless optimism and hope for our future success is a mental prison. It's good to keep going. Does this mean there are "good" mental prisons? Maybe.

As we strive for balance between optimism and self-awareness, let's remember that our mental prisons are not always bad things. Sometimes they're necessary frameworks for growth and progress (as long as they're short-lived). There will be times we over-promise and under-deliver, but it should not be our M.O.

"Only" $30,000 per month

Before I started my own business, the idea of making $5,000 per month with my own business was preposterous. Why on earth would anyone give me $5,000 per month? It seemed insane to me. Yet, the agency I worked for at the time was charging customers at least $185 per hour for my time. That's a lot more than a $5K/month rate!

I started my business in 2020 and quickly brought in $15K/month in sales. A few months later, the business was making $20K/month. That's when I quit my day job and went full time. $20K sounded like a lot of money, but after payroll, taxes, and expenses, I was "only" able to pay myself $5K/month plus healthcare benefits.

Unfortunately, $5K/month isn't enough to pay the bills for a family of five, so I had to start selling more. I brought the top line revenue to $30K/month and we hired someone. We had cash flow issues, so to combat that, I got our revenue to $40K/month. That was nice, but we had to hire another person to help with the work, so I got the revenue to $50K/month.

Do you see where this is going?

The goalposts were always moving and I'd forgotten about my initial doubts of being able to generate $5,000 in a month. I gave myself no credit. At $50K/month, I was actually feeling pretty good, but then AI hit the market and my cash flow fell apart.

Despite 10X'ing my "impossible" $5,000 milestone, I always felt behind. Was I a failure? Or a 10X achiever? I'll let you figure out how I felt.

PRISON MINDSET

"But, you're not in prison"

See those two goofballs up there? You and I are one of them. Sure, we may look different, but they are our spiritual and psychological brother and sister. Just like them, we are voluntarily carrying around prison bars. Maybe we've even decorated them and grown to love them.

But those bars are death. They make us prisoners of our own minds.

We know those bars are bad for us, yet we still hang on to them. Willingly.

It has nothing to do with data, evidence, or scientific evidence. It's to do with our emotions and the way our human brains work in meat space.

I didn't believe it myself until I read a neuroscience book called Descartes' Error, which contained the key quote on the next page (one of the most important concepts in this whole book)...

MENTAL PRISONS

We aren't thinking machines. We are feeling machines that think.

– Antonio Damasio,
Descartes' Error

Feeling bad feels good

It sucks that this is true, but sometimes feeling bad just... feels good. Entrepreneurs love the day-to-day "hustle and grind." We've wired ourselves to equate discomfort with progress. So when we're not feeling miserable, we start wondering if we're doing it wrong. No pain, no gain, right?

We beat ourselves up for not shipping faster. For not scaling sooner. For not closing that deal. For spending $3,000 on a marketing consultant who gave us a PDF. And instead of shrugging it off and moving on, we marinate in the shame. We relish it. Because deep down, we think it's what we deserve.

But not because we're victims.

There's a weird ego boost in self-loathing. It sounds twisted, but if I tell myself I suck, I get to feel like I'm holding myself to a higher standard. Like I'm the only one smart enough to see how bad I really am. That's not humility. That's pride in disguise.

As entrepreneurs, we're used to taking responsibility for everything. That's part of the job. But there's a difference between taking responsibility and becoming your own emotional punching bag. One moves the business forward. The other keeps you locked in a cycle of guilt and self-flagellation.

This is one of the nastiest mental prisons: the belief that you have to feel bad in order to do good. That if you're not suffering, you're slacking. And if you start to feel good, you must be missing something.

Call me crazy, but maybe we don't need to feel bad to feel good.

The myth of the successful solopreneur

The solo founder myth is seductive. One genius, bootstrapping their way from idea to empire. No help, no breaks, just pure hustle and vision. Sounds awesome, except that it's total fiction. (Yes, there are exceptions to the rule, but for every self-made millionaire, there are thousands of people who tried it and failed. 99.9% of entrepreneurs need help from other people.)

Don't perpetuate the lie by being the entrepreneur who acts like they should be a 1-person show. It only exists because it's a revisionist-history version of what actually happens.

Even the most successful "solo" entrepreneurs had help from mentors, spouses, contractors, silent partners, generous friends, and former colleagues who handed them their first big deal. But the version that makes headlines is cleaner, simpler, and more heroic.

So we end up trying to be the design department, sales team, bookkeeper, writer, strategist, project manager, executive assistant, and therapist—all at once. And when we inevitably drop a ball, we beat ourselves up like we're failing at a job that actually takes five people to do well.

You don't get extra credit for doing it all alone. You only get tired, bitter, and isolated. No investor or customer is going to say, "Wow, you burned yourself out trying to do everything. That's leadership!"

As long as you're clinging to the 1-person show idea, you're holding onto a mental prison labeled "I have to do this alone." You don't and you never did.

Even Batman had Alfred.

When did I pick up these bars?

After I realized I'd been holding these mental prison bars, I had to ask myself when I first picked them up. Was there an event that triggered it? Did I inherit it from my parents? Or maybe someone else "gave them to me?"

My earliest mental prison memory is from when I was nine years old. It's embarrassing to admit, but I picked up the habit of typing the following sentence on computer keyboards as a kid:

Anthony Garone is the stupidest kid in the whole world and we know this is true because it is in the Guinness Book of World Records.

That sentence hit on my three of my favorite things: immaturity, humor, and inflicting pain. And over time, I could type it really, really fast.

Every time I made a mistake, missed a question on a test, or took a bad photograph, it reinforced that I was the "stupidest kid in the world," even if it wasn't actually in the Guinness Book of World Records.

I refused to believe that mistakes were a normal part of everyday life, or that other people made as many "dumb" mistakes as I did. My self talk sounded like, "Oh, you made another mistake? You really are a stupid idiot." For me, mistakes were a symptom of being a walking failure. By doing this, I'd given myself a life sentence in a mental prison.

Thankfully, I don't type that sentence anymore, but when I find myself back in that "stupidest in the world" mindset, I remind myself what those steel bars feel like in my fingers.

The "spotlight effect"

In pop psychology, there's something called the "spotlight effect," which says that everyone falsely believes that the world is paying close attention to them. For example, if you walked down the street wearing a shirt with a mustard stain, people would absolutely notice and think you're a slob. As nonsensical as that is, it's exactly how our social brains work.

The more I thought about this effect, the more I questioned it. If everyone's so worried about everyone else, how much "stuff" can I get away with? The contrarian part of me just had to know.

My first experiments were with emails. I eliminated greetings ("Hi Jimmy") and closures ("Have a great weekend"). Nobody seemed to notice or care.

Then I moved on to YouTube videos. I'd make mistakes and leave them in. Nobody seemed to notice or care.

Then I moved on to Twitter/X. I posted things that I would have thought too silly or embarrassing. Fewer people liked those posts, but my account didn't suffer in any way.

All this led me to adopt the mantra, "Done is better than perfect." It took me about a year to realize I could make plenty of mistakes, enjoy myself, and no one would know (or care about) the difference.

This was a big step toward freedom.

Ash Lamb on the spotlight effect

Used with permission. © Ash Lamb, ashlamb.com

Pick your prison persona

Entrepreneurship attracts dysfunction, then rewards it. Over time, we all develop our own unique flavor, and we get really good at justifying it. Below are a few mental prison archetypes I've seen (and lived). If you recognize yourself in one (or all) of them, congrats. You're in good company.

The Martyr "If I'm not suffering, I'm not doing it right."

Wears burnout like a badge. Thinks rest is laziness. Always grinding, never satisfied. Believes work is only legit if it's paid for in blood, sweat, and spirals.

The Pivot Addict "If I keep reinventing, I'll eventually land on perfection."

Builds momentum and immediately shifts gears. Confuses novelty with progress. Treats boredom as failure. Thinks clarity is a trap.

The Overthinker "If I give it some more thought, I'll figure it out."

Endless planning, minimal action. Reads a ton, starts nothing. Obsesses over frameworks and thought leadership, but gets paralyzed when it's time to ship.

The Control Freak "If I don't do it, it'll never get done right."

Won't delegate. Micromanages. Builds everything from scratch because "off-the-shelf stuff sucks." Proud of independence but secretly drowning in tasks.

The Ghost "If I go quiet for long enough, the problem will solve itself."

Disappears when it's time for hard conversations with clients, partners, employees, or even themselves. Avoids conflict, accountability, or commitment.

The Scarcity Hoarder "There's never enough, so I have to hold on tight."

operates like the next sale might be the last one... ever. Hoards cash. Avoids hiring. Undersells out of fear the client will walk. Says yes to bad-fit projects because "we need the money."

PRISON MINDSET: MAIN IDEAS

A mental prison is a strongly held self-limiting belief that undermines your business.

☞ Certainty and knowledge are feelings, not facts.

☞ Negative self-talk is the first and most obvious symptom of a mental prison.

☞ The "spotlight effect" means everyone else is caught up in their own head.

☞ Entrepreneurs carry fear long after it's needed. If we never stop to question it, we build our businesses from a prison cell.

Mental prison gut-check

What is freedom?

- Define "freedom." If I was free of my mental prisons, what would it look like?

- What old habits would end?

- What new habits would begin?

- Which habits would I continue?

- Is there someone who embodies my definition of "freedom?" Who and why?

Who else can solve my problems?

- Think about the biggest problems with my self-esteem and self-talk. What got me to each of these problems?

- How much of what got me to each problem was my fault?

- How much of what got me to each problem was someone else's fault?

- Do I have any potential solutions to my problems? If so, can someone else solve them?

I can do this, right?

- Who are 5-10 people I admire?

- What is it about each of them that I admire?

- What do they "do" (i.e. what's their profession, how do they spend their time?

- Could I have ended up with their abilities and admirable qualities? Why?

- Could I have ended up in their position (inner peace, professional status, wealth, mindset, skills, etc.)? Why?

- Do they have problems in their own lives? If so, how are those problems solved?

- Do I know enough to answer these questions?

*Busy is a choice.
Stress is a choice.
Giving yourself to joy is a choice.
Choose well.*

– Ann Voskamp

CHAPTER TWO

Feeling Machines

FEELING MACHINES

Feeling machines that think

I hate to break it to you, but you are not rational. It's okay, I'm not rational, either. No, it's not because we're entrepreneurs. It's because you and I are humans. And humans—bless our sweet, little hearts—are irrational.

We want to believe we're rational "thinking machines" and we're always making the smartest decisions based on facts, judgment, and insights, but the neuroscience says otherwise.

When Dr. Antonio Damasio wrote that we're "feeling machines that think," he showed how people with damaged emotional centers in their brain couldn't even make simple decisions. Thankfully, their logic still worked fine. His book Descartes' Error is full of examples and evidence that we "feel" our way to a decision and then rationalize it after the fact.

Even crazier: according to neurologist Robert A. Burton, "knowledge" and "certainty" are just more of that "feeling machine" stuff. They're emotions, too, like anger and pride. In his book, On Being Certain: Believing You Are Right Even When You're Not, he tells story after story that back up his claim. (Don't believe it? Just re-read that book title, bucko.)

You might ask yourself, "Well if that's true, then how do I know what I know?" Well, you don't! You feel you know what you know and that feeling is enough to make you believe you're right—even if you're not.

Once you realize your brain is running on emotion-first logic, you can stop pretending you're a hyper-rational decision-making machine and start building tools, habits, and environments that account for your irrationality.

So, we're all improvising our way through entrepreneurship. Feeling first, thinking second, and rationalizing third. But once you know that, you can start noticing the bars of your mental prison.

MENTAL PRISONS

Customers are feeling machines, too

The big secret to sales and marketing is to identify the language that attracts your potential customers, resonates with their needs, and convinces them to hand you money. The best way to do that is to remember that, like you, they are feeling machines that think.

Whether they're buying a half-million dollar tractor, a 6-month engagement with a fractional CMO, or a kitchen remodel, they're still making emotional buying decisions and rationalizing them afterwards.

I bring this up because I've worked with so many founders who have the "if I build it, they will come" mindset around their business. This idea is a mental prison. The free market doesn't run on meritocracy and the best product does not always win. You will not be successful because you've built "the best" widget or you're "the best" at what you do.

You will be successful because you've effectively marketed and sold your products and services to feeling machines using the language they need to make a buying decision.

This should make perfect sense to you because it's exactly how you and I operate. If I have a water pipe burst in my home at 2AM, I'm going to online and look for "emergency 24/7 plumber in Phoenix, Arizona." And I will call the first company whose website says "Call at any hour for any reason for fast, reliable service." That's the language that meets me exactly where I am.

You, your customers, and I all operate this way. Do not discount this fact. If you do, you'll lose sleep at night wondering why no one is buying from you, why you have no sales pipeline, and whether you'll still be in business.

Practice running a healthy business

Processes are a big part of feeling machine behavior. No matter what you do, no matter who you are, no matter your level of expertise—you have a process and you repeat it daily. Sure, you may make some tweaks here and there, and some days it's faster or slower than others, but it's still a repeatable thing you've practiced and know how to do.

Let me bring your attention to the word "practiced." Any thing you do more than once is a practice. You can practice anything, from a learning a song on a musical instrument to stubbing your pinky toe on the same dining room chair every month. It doesn't matter what it is. If you can repeat it, you can practice it.

You can also practice how you respond to your emotions. For example, every time you lose a customer, you can practice freaking out or taking it in stride. In fact, you can practice it to the point of habituation, when it becomes a practically-involuntary response.

This gets to one of the most important quotes I've ever come across:

> **Practice does not make perfect.**
>
> **Perfect practice makes perfect.**
>
> – *Vince Lombardi, American football coach*

As a business owner, I've observed the processes I follow that have led to habituated mistakes. When a sales prospect asks, "Is there any way you can cut your costs?" I usually say, "Yes. I think we can do that." Then a week later, I am kicking myself because I know I'm going to lose money by discounting the work because I'm too desperate to win the prospect.

Instead, I have established new processes, like fixed minimum pricing and only offering discounts if the prospect buys in bulk. Perfect practice making perfect.

Don't trust feelings or spreadsheets

Conventional wisdom says to "trust your heart" or "go with your gut." Well, what if your heart and gut lead you to build a business that feels more like a prison than a way to financial freedom?

Susan David's book Emotional Agility provided this incredibly simple insight:

Feelings are data, not facts.

I learned this lesson the hard way from a teacher of the Alexander Technique (AT). If you don't know, AT teaches you how to use your body well. It covers posture, bending over, sitting, standing, walking, breathing, and more. (Do a search for "psychophysical reeducation" or read the book Body Language by Michael Gelb.)

The AT teacher asked me to look straight ahead, which I did—or at least I thought I did. He pushed my chin down and adjusted the angle of my skull on my neck. I said, "That doesn't feel right." He said, "Your feelings are wrong. You can't trust them. Now that I've adjusted you, you're actually looking straight ahead."

If I can't assess whether my head is literally on straight, then how can I assess the health of my business? Believing something to be true does not make it true, no matter what the spreadsheet says. I'm reminded of a joke:

A CEO asked his CFO, "How do the numbers look?" The CFO replied, "How do you want them to look?"

How do your numbers look?

Finding yourself through mistakes

Michael Manring is one of the most innovative bassists in the world. When he was younger, he idolized the legendary jazz bassist Jaco Pastorius. Eventually, he went on to take lessons from Jaco himself while studying at the prestigious Berklee College of Music in Boston.

Having studied Jaco's playing so deeply, Michael was convinced, saying, "Nobody's ever going to do better than Jaco. The best you can do is just emulate him and try to do it in a good and respectable way."

In his lessons with Jaco, there were some performance elements he "couldn't get" and Michael instead played "the wrong things" that didn't fit Jaco's style. It took him a while to realize "that those 'mistakes' I was making weren't actually real mistakes. That was me! I was never going to be able to play like him because I wasn't him."

Michael had spent so much time focusing on sounding like Jaco that he ignored all the playing that didn't sound like Jaco until he realized it was his own sound emerging in his playing.

Over time, Michael came to see other issues in Jaco's life that he didn't want to emulate. He said, "If that's the kind of person you have to be to make really good music, it's not worth it."

After a while, he realized, "That's just not me and those little 'mistakes' when I'd try to play his music, those things were never going to go away—and they shouldn't because all those little things are me. So I'd try to turn it around and develop those things instead of just trying to get rid of them from my music."

Mental Prison self-talk

The language we use to talk about (and with) ourselves is a primary indicator of the quality of our linguistic practice. For myself, I had to first develop awareness that I was using unhealthy language about myself before I could change the process and practice of talking about (and with) myself.

The more I listened to what I said about myself, the more I heard self-limiting and diminishing language. I often talked about what I couldn't do, what I didn't have, and what I didn't deserve. Here's a table demonstrating some of that language:

Mental prison self-talk classifications

Types of Language	Examples
Comparative	"I'm not as…" "He/She is so much better at…"
Judgmental	"I'm too…" "I could never…"
Fearful	"I'd love to, but…" "I really wish I could…"
Fatalistic	"I'll never be able to…" "Too bad I'll always be…" "I have to…"
Outlandish	"I suck." "I should just quit." "I'm the worst."
Predictive	"If I just get this done…" "I'll be happy once I…"
Overly-Critical	"I hate that I…" "I hate my…"

"I could never write a book"

The mental prisons self-talk classifications helped me identify my self-limiting language patterns and habits. I grew a deeper awareness of when I used them and started nipping the problem in the bud. It took a few months before I stopped using that type of language altogether.

Going through the exercise helped me to see that most people speak in these ways. In fact, I was meeting with a friend of mine and we were talking about one of my books. He said, "I could never write a book." I asked why. He replied, "I'm just not smart enough and don't have enough to say."

I said to him, "Yeah, but you're really good at sales. Couldn't you talk about that for a couple of hours straight?" He replied, "Oh yeah, I could go all day."

I said, "See, you could write a book."

Then he realized he actually is smart enough and has enough to say. He nodded and said, "Yeah, I guess you're right. I probably could write a book."

How to sell to feeling machines

Since I primarily work with technical companies, I do a lot of marketing consulting on persona development, messaging, and positioning. Tech companies want to wow the world with incredible features, unbelievable scalability, and killer pricing.

Unfortunately, nobody cares about tech companies until they have a reason to. And many tech companies don't give people a reason to.

Most tech companies look at the world like it's full of thinking machines. They use technical jargon and useless tactics that don't convince customers to want to buy. Worse, they forget that most people don't want to be sold to. Buyers today increasingly want to make buying decisions on their own by: 1. Doing research, and 2. Never, ever talking to a salesperson.

Yet entrepreneurs must sell, and so many of them are just so, so bad at it. The quality of a product doesn't matter as much as how the product (and its packaging) makes someone feel. OMG, I really wish people could grok this.

As an entrepreneur myself, I've had to lean on other people to show me where I'm acting like a thinking machine, even in my own marketing. In fact, only two weeks ago, I received advice from a couple of successful friends that helped me see my business so much more clearly than before. I've run it for almost five years now and having made nearly $2M since launch and I still didn't see it.

Selling to feeling machines requires getting out of our own heads and getting into the heads of our prospects and future customers. Once I started understanding the "spotlight effect" and my all-too-common mental prisons, the more clearly I could see paths to success for my company.

☞ In a mental prison, it's easier to believe in brainwashing than your own actual capabilities.

☞ Everything can be practiced, from breathing to spreadsheets.

☞ We think we're rational, but we're actually driven by emotion.

☞ Your feelings are real, but they are not reliable sources of truth.

FEELING MACHINES: MAIN IDEAS

Mental prison gut-check

The path toward "escaping" mental prisons is loaded with questions and activity. The original draft of this book included more than 1,000 questions I asked myself along the way. Instead of inundating you with all that, here are some key questions that help me to see clearly:

- What am I doing to cause myself to unnecessarily suffer?
- When do I feel like I need to suffer to succeed?
- What "milestone" am I chasing that might not actually matter?
- What compliment or success am I still refusing to believe?
- What's something I won't let go of even though it's clearly not working?
- What story about myself do I keep repeating that might be total BS?
- If I wasn't running this business, would I still like/hate myself?
- Do I measure my success by revenue, relevance, or something else?
- Who am I trying to impress and do they care?
- Am I building a business that serves my goals or one that looks good on LinkedIn?
- Is "busy" my default personality trait? Is that something I want?
- Will money (or success) solve this problem? Or any of my problems?
- What part of my business scares me the most and why?
- What does "freedom" mean to me?

Practice does not make perfect. Perfect practice makes perfect.

– Vince Lombardi

CHAPTER THREE

COMPLIMENTS

My friends: *Dude, you're so smart.*

My wife: *I'm so proud of you.*

My parents: *You're so successful.*

My customers: *You do awesome work!*

My 40,000 YouTube subscribers: *This is the best channel ever!*

Me: *I'm a failure.*

Liars, suckers, or truth-tellers

Receiving compliments is the worst, isn't it? It is truly terrible. You have to go through that whole "Oh, thank you. You're too generous" song and dance just to avoid having to face those dreadful kind words. On the outside, it's all smiles. On the inside, you're wondering how much it would hurt to jump through that nearby window.

Or, maybe you're like I was and believe you're astonishingly good at tricking smart and wonderful people into doing foolish things like hiring you for a good salary, being your friend, helping you move, giving you gifts, or getting married to you. The world is full of suckers!

In my mental prison, I was both an idiot and a persuasive genius! *This is how ridiculous the mental prison mindset is.* Because I was such a believer in my own BS, I'd use clichés like: "God is good!" or "Hey, a broken clock is right twice a day," or "Chalk it up to dumb luck."

But here's where things got tricky: I got so good at my work that it started reaching my heroes. I'm not talking about the C-level exec I really respect—I'm talking about my heroes that I read about in magazines as a teenager.

Two of my lifelong guitar heroes watched my guitar videos on YouTube and told me I was great. At that point, I had a really difficult choice to make:

Either my heroes are liars and they're just being nice,

or they're suckers like everyone else, or

(worst case scenario) they are telling me the truth.

MENTAL PRISONS

How criticism affects cash flow

Criticism is easy to give and hard to receive, especially when you're building something of your own. Everyone thinks their opinion is the hard truth. But most of the time, it's just noise. Like the old joke: "Opinions are like buttholes. Everyone has one, and they think the others stink."

I try not to take criticism seriously unless it comes from someone I respect: a customer, an expert, or someone who's done what I'm trying to do. Otherwise, it's usually not worth sorting through.

That includes my own opinions. A lot of them were handed to me, not earned. I've had strong takes about people I've never met and decisions I've never had to make. Most of us do.

In business, this gets dangerous. I've ignored solid advice because I didn't feel confident enough to act on it. One example: my friend Karl Hughes, a successful entrepreneur who runs several successful companies, once told me I needed to tighten up my up-front payment terms. I agreed, but didn't enforce it.

To be honest, I felt anxious to do it and avoided the problem for months.

The result? Cash flow headaches, stress, and close calls on payroll. If I'd acted instead of overthinking, I could've saved myself a lot of pain.

Feedback only helps if you're ready to do something with it. And readiness starts with mindset.

Impostor syndrome or mental prison?

I used to think I had impostor syndrome. I'd get praise from clients, subscribers, friends—heck, even my heroes—and immediately think, "They're being nice." Or worse, "They're idiots."

But over time, I realized it wasn't impostor syndrome. It was something deeper and dumber: I believed I was actually bad at what I did. Not "fooling people" bad. Just objectively bad.

> **Impostor syndrome says, "I'm no good and I worry people will find out."**
>
> **Mental prison says, "I'm no good and everyone's just confused."**

One is a fear of being exposed. The other is a desire to be saved.

As a mental prisoner, I didn't need people to stop doubting me. They had to convince me I wasn't garbage, which isn't impostor syndrome. I'd actually call it a prison I built on fake humility.

As I wrestled with this issue in my life, I had to ask myself: Am I afraid people will find out the truth? Or am I hoping someone will finally prove me wrong?

I knew my problem wasn't impostor syndrome when I saw the legendary guitar virtuoso Allan Holdsworth perform live in 2014. After every song, he'd reach for the microphone, insult himself, and apologize to the audience for his poor performance. "That was Farmer Al on the banjo, still figuring out how to pluck the strings. I'm so sorry. You really deserve better than this."

Thankfully, the audience encouraged him all night. They knew they were watching a genius at work, even if the genius hated himself.

Coping with compliments

My relationship status with compliments has always been "awkward." It's always much easier to give a compliment than to receive one, especially with a mental prison mindset because I rarely thought I deserved them.

A meaningful compliment is a narrative violation in the mental prison. For example, "How could someone say something kind to me when I'm clearly an idiot?" Here are the ways I deflected and avoided compliments in order to cope with the awkwardness I experienced receiving them. Do you do these, too?

- **Change the subject:** Act like the compliment never happened. Simply smile, nod, and quickly think of something else to talk about. "Thank you! So, what's going on in your world?"

- **Return the favor:** This treats the compliment like a game of ping pong. Someone serves, you return. After receiving a compliment, say something like, "Oh that's really nice of you!" and then make something favorable up on the spot about the other person.

- **Downplay:** This was my favorite go-to and the easiest one to pull off. Start with, "Thanks, but…" and take it from there.

- **Make it a joke:** Turn that compliment into something you both can enjoy. "Hah! I'll send you $10 every time you say that about me!"

These and other strategies are incredibly useful for people who never want to give up their mental prisons.

And if you catch someone else using them, don't let them get away with it. I will literally say, "Oh no, you don't. I know all the tactics for avoiding a compliment. I am telling you the truth, not blowing smoke up your butt." (Also, why is that a saying?)

Accepting a compliment

Instead of awkwardly accepting compliments with cheesy one-liners like "Oh you're too kind," I've gone through a bit of work to actually **listen** to compliments, **acknowledge** them with gratitude, **accept** them, and **internalize** them so I continue to improve while staying humble.

- **Listening** to a compliment is an essential first step. People don't dole out compliments willy nilly. If someone is going to speak into my life, I give them my full attention. Phones down, distractions put away.

- **Acknowledging** a compliment is simple. If a compliment is received in person, make eye contact and say, "Thank you." Often, I will also explain why I'm grateful for the compliment. For example, "Thank you for recognizing the hard work I've done. I often hope others see the value in what I do as you just did."

- **Accepting** a compliment is not a visible action, but an intentional decision to remember the compliment, the complimenter, and the context in which I received it.

- **Internalizing** a compliment is a process of integration. When I internalize a compliment, it becomes another piece of evidence I use to counter a negative internal thought or a drive-by jerkwad spewing dumb comments.

- As an entrepreneur, I will sometimes go one step further and ask if I can publish the compliment on my business website as feedback, or ask if the person wouldn't mind filling in a feedback form to memorialize their words. It's not for my benefit, but so I can honor their words with an actual placement on my website.

COMPLIMENTS: MAIN IDEAS

☞ **Compliments often feel like lies when you're stuck in a mental prison.**

☞ **If you can't internalize positive feedback, you'll stay trapped in negative self-perception, no matter how well your business is doing.**

☞ **Most entrepreneurs don't know how to receive praise.**

☞ **Entrepreneurs need to accept compliments as real data and not delusions.**

Mental prison gut check

These are questions I've asked myself about compliments. They're not easy to answer because they call into question ego, pride, and a sense of significance.

- What is my exact thought process when I receive a compliment?
- Do I internally enjoy receiving compliments?
- Do I externally enjoy receiving compliments?
- What was the last compliment I received?
- How did that compliment make me feel?
- Do I believe that compliment to be true?
- Why did I receive that compliment?
- Is that compliment similar to others I've received? If so, why might that be?
- Are there compliments I've received in the past that I do not believe are true?
- Why do I have trouble believing compliments from other people? Is it me or is it the person offering the compliment?
- Do I enjoy providing compliments?
- What are some of the most recent compliments I've given and to whom?
- Did I have any ulterior motives offering them?
- What is the most honest and authentic compliment I've given someone? How did I feel at the time? Why did I offer it?
- Have I ever offered a compliment that I felt was taken honestly and seriously? Was that more to do with me or the recipient?
- Am I someone whose compliments should be taken seriously? Why?
- What are my motivations about giving compliments?

CHAPTER FOUR

Mind Control

MENTAL PRISONS

How beliefs become business strategy

Your mindset is so much more than a private voice in your head. It's actually reflected in your roadmap, pricing, org chart, positioning, goals, and calendar.

If you believe you're not worth high-ticket clients, you'll keep undercharging. Over time, the gap between your price and market value will continue to increase and you'll find yourself on a treadmill that's continuously speeding up. (Ask me how I know.)

If you think you're not ready to lead, you'll avoid hiring or cling to every decision. Then you'll fall for the sunk cost fallacy, thinking, "I already spent six months and tons of revenue on this. If I don't continue, it'll all go to waste."

If you secretly doubt you're good at what you do, your marketing will stay vague, cautious, or nonexistent. Trust me, "We're really good at what we do" won't convince a single prospect to convert.

This is how beliefs become business strategy without you even realizing it.

Business owners build systems to reinforce your comfort zone. Then they design around fear instead of potential. And the results show it.

The worst part? From the outside, it might look like everything is all right. But over time, the business evolves into something the owner never intended and your inner saboteur thinks is "safe."

Mind control messes with your head and shapes the whole business.

Mental prisoners aren't tricking customers into buying. We trick ourselves into selling out.

Bad beliefs become company culture

Beliefs shape the business, whether you mean for them to or not. Your team follows your strategy and absorbs your fears, too.

If you're unsure or wishy-washy about pricing because you can never say "no" to work, they'll hesitate when quoting. Then if you avoid narrowing your focus, they'll overextend to chase whatever work they can find.

If you're quietly afraid to let go of "good" customers, your entire sales process will optimize for comfort, not growth.

At a previous company, we hovered right around $8M in annual revenue for several years. Everyone wanted to break $10M, but it never happened. Why? We were proud of our broad customer base and flexible service model. We were too proud to admit we were being vague.

We couldn't target higher-value clients without narrowing our focus, and we weren't willing to do that. Years after I left, the company got more specific with their positioning and finally crossed the $10M line.

Even at the 7-figure level, fear of change can cap your potential. That inside DIY mind control job starts branching out to your team and your organization. Scary.

Your team can only scale as far as your beliefs allow them to. If you want them to think bigger, you have to go first. And if you're reading this book, it probably means you have to let go of the bars.

If I'm so smart, why am I unhappy?

Life in a mental prison is riddled with nonsensical contradictions. On the one hand, I could be a successful, well-paid expert who deserved a bigger salary, a loftier title, and a nicer office. On the other hand, I had tricked a bunch of people into hiring a moron to do high-value work for them.

In my mental prison, I was both a genius and an idiot. A high performer and a loser. Happily married to a beautiful, intelligent woman, yet somehow I was also ugly and stupid. It didn't make sense because it didn't need to. In a mental prison, anything goes—as long as it makes me feel bad about myself.

At some point I realized that I must have been a master manipulator to have so many friends who liked me, coworkers who respected me, fellow musicians who wanted to work with me, and customers who wanted to buy from me.

Or, God forbid, I was actually a likable, respectable, and trustworthy person. Let's just say that wasn't true. Then I must be incredibly smart to trick all those likable, respectable, and trustworthy people I actually liked. But being smart is a narrative violation of the mental prison.

So, what's the truth? Master at controlling other people's minds or just a quality person?

This is the ultimate question for a mental prisoner.

So many successful entrepreneurs question themselves, wonder whether they should continue, and fear failure. They lack confidence and focus on negativity. They're somehow optimistic and hopeless. A walking contradiction.

The person holding the bars

In the TV show The Prisoner (the 1968 show that inspired this book), the main character offers this heavy statement:

"I am not a number. I am a person."

As a mental prisoner, it's easy to forget that. We get so used to gripping the bars and seeing life through them that we forget we're the ones holding them in the first place.

The longer we live that way, the more it becomes our default. We stop questioning the limitations. We start believing the stories. We mistake the bars for reality.

But your life isn't the limited view. It isn't the fear of being exposed, or the self-doubt that whispers you're not enough. That's not truth. That's programming. Behind those bars is a uniquely-created person with once-in-a-universe DNA and an opportunity to do something unusual.

The world doesn't need more entrepreneurs holding prison bars. It needs more entrepreneurs living lives of creative freedom without impostor syndrome, shame, and the belief they've "tricked" everyone into thinking they're competent.

You're (hopefully!) not a fraud. You're not a number. You're not stuck.

You're holding prison bars you created. You can put them down.

Failure is one of those things that 'serious people' dread. Invariably, the persons most likely to be crippled by this fear are people who have convinced themselves that they are SO bitchen they shouldn't ever be placed in a situation where they might fail.

– Frank Zappa

The importance of failure

Failure is an "f-word" that most people hate. It's such a difficult word that people are redefining it. You'll usually hear it in the context of Silicon Valley product development: "Fail fast, fail forward" or "Move fast and break things."

Real failure (also known as "ruin") is most certainly a bad thing. Do not pursue it. You do not need to fail your way into bankruptcy, burn out your team, or destroy your marriage in the name of growth. But this other kind of failure (the small, honest kind) is something worth pursuing.

The problem is, most of us don't know how to separate ruin from learning. We hear "failure" and immediately picture public embarrassment, angry customers, revenue drops, or the shame of admitting we were wrong. That's not failure. That's ego reacting to feedback.

Failure, in the way I'm talking about it, is simply trying something that doesn't work. It's feedback. It's information. It's proof you did something instead of endlessly thinking about doing something.

When I look back at the most useful moments in my career, they almost always include failure. Failed pitches. Failed product launches. Failed experiments. But each one gave me data, perspective, and confidence that I wouldn't have gained otherwise.

Here's the catch: failure only matters if you're willing to face it. Not just spin it or reframe it as "a pivot" or "a win in disguise." But actually sit with it and say, "That didn't work. I wonder why."

That's when failure becomes useful. That's when it becomes growth.

Embracing failure

Entrepreneurs love to talk about failure in theory—usually right after they've "come out on the other side." But when it's happening in real time? Nobody's posting about that.

We don't celebrate failure. We survive it. Going out of business, losing a key client, making a dumb financial decision. These are not Instagram-worthy moments. They're stressful, humbling, and sometimes deeply embarrassing.

But a few years ago, I decided to stop pretending I was above it. I launched a YouTube series called Failure to Fracture as a public documentation of me trying to learn one of the most difficult guitar pieces ever written: King Crimson's Fracture. The whole point was to show the process, not the perfection. I knew I'd screw up. I knew it would be messy. That was the point.

Every missed note, every frustrated sigh, every "I thought I had this!" moment—it's all there. And you know what? People loved it. Not because I failed, but because I showed the failure. Because it made the eventual progress feel earned. The series has more than half a million views.

Making those videos taught me something I carry into my business: failure is only shameful when it's hidden. If you let it breathe, if you're honest about it, it becomes something else entirely. It becomes proof that you're still learning. Still swinging. Still building.

I don't chase failure, but I don't hide from it anymore either. I let it teach me. I let it remind me I'm human. And then I get back to work.

Learn from failures or risk repeating them

Failure hurts, but it's never the problem. Repeating failure is the problem. And boy have I been there on multiple occasions.

Every failed launch, missed deadline, bad hire, or cash flow crunch comes with data. But if you don't slow down long enough to look at it, you miss the whole point and set yourself up to do it again.

For example, I've hired people to fill in my gaps and I simply expected them to jump right in to fix everything. Unfortunately, they can't read my mind, they don't know where the gaps are, and they don't want to be sent on a voyage of discovery. So, I end up spending money on people, set them up to fail, let them go, and waste everyone's time and money.

Thankfully, I've learned the lesson and have stopped doing that, but I've easily lost $50K on this mental prison behavior.

Failure isn't something to move past as quickly as possible. Entrepreneurs frequently brush it off, tell themselves it was bad luck, or blame the wrong variable. That's not resilience. It's denial with good branding.

Failure is expensive, so don't waste the opportunity to learn and correct.

Ask: What did I do? What actually happened? What would I do differently next time?

If you don't pull meaning out of it, you'll keep paying tuition without getting the lesson.

"My employees suck"

This story is based on a true story. Details have been anonymized for obvious reasons. Don't ask. :)

A CEO friend of mine was having trouble with his sales team. They were successful at getting initial conversations going with prospects, but nothing ever led to closed contracts. In other words, the sales team was costing a lot more than they were making.

The CEO said to me, "Why does every salesperson suck nowadays?" I replied, "What do you mean? Why do they suck?"

"Well, they're supposed to be making me money. Instead, I'm paying them a lot of money to travel and buy expensive dinners." I replied, "Ouch. What do you mean 'every sales person?'"

"This is my third consecutive sales team with this problem!" I said, "What?! How'd these guys get hired?"

He said, "I hired them." I asked why he'd hire three consecutive sucky sales teams, which he didn't like. "Well, they didn't suck in their previous roles!"

I asked, "If they didn't suck in their prior roles, why do they suck now?" He said, "I don't know. I'm going to fire them."

One of the sales guys reached out to me later by coincidence. I asked how things were going for him. "Man, not good. We're not closing any deals because we have no collateral, we get zero direction from above, we have no ads, we do no marketing, and none of our services are specific."

It never occurred to my CEO friend that he could be the reason his sales team sucks. The chances of three once-successful sales teams suddenly failing is pretty low.

☞ Your thoughts can't always be trusted. They're often influenced by past programming.

☞ If you don't take control of your mind, someone or something else will.

☞ Your environment shapes your beliefs far more than you think.

☞ You can't escape mental prisons without first noticing the scripts running in your head.

Mental prison gut check

To actually learn the lessons of failure, we must take an honest assessment of our successes and where we went wrong. Here are some questions I work through to help me see where I may be wrong, even about my failures.

- What do I actively and intentionally practice?
- Why do I practice? Do I have a sense of getting "better" or am I looking for something less serious, like "increasing my skills?"
- What's the difference between how I currently practice and "perfect practice?"
- Have I ever considered a coach or a teacher to help me practice?
- How would I rate myself on a scale from 1 to 10 for each of the activities or skills I practice?
- Do I know enough to evaluate what a 10 is on that scale?
- How much time have I spent practicing each skill?
- Where did I learn how to practice?
- Is my practice routine effective? Does it help me to make progress?
- How am I evaluating whether I am progressing?
- Do I have a repeatable, structured practice routine? Or do I wing it?
- Have I ever had a "failed" or "ineffective" practice session? What made me feel it was a failure?
- When was my last great practice session? What made it great? What was I working on at the time?
- Am I practiced enough to call myself an "expert" or "professional?" How would I know?

Sometimes my mind is destructive to myself. We are our own worst enemies.

– Kielyn Marrone,
Alone (TV Series)

CHAPTER FIVE

MONDAYS

MENTAL PRISONS

A case of the Mondays

Isn't it crazy that a huge number of people wake up every Monday to do something they hate? And it's not just a few hours every Monday, but dozens of hours every day of the week! It's bonkers.

To escape the corporate grind, many of us start our own businesses, seeking freedom, autonomy, control, and a better shot at wealth. We are lucky to live in a time where starting a business requires nothing more than a computer and internet access. Welcome to life in the future!

And yet, I know entrepreneurs who hate their day-to-day work experience. They've created a company that's become a mental prison. It dominates their schedule, their thought life, and their relationships. They can't blame their boss or their customers or anyone else. There's no one else in control. They can change it if they want to, but they feel helpless.

The hard truth is that it's not the job, but the person working it.

Here's how I look at it: I can be miserable running my business 50 hours a week or I can be miserable working for someone else 50 hours a week. The problem isn't the 50 hours a week or who I'm working for. The problem is me, for I am the maker of my misery.

Sure, you could argue that "the work" is the source of misery, but I'd probably be even more miserable 50 hours a week if I didn't have a job.

Having "a case of the Mondays" isn't about the job, the day of the week, or the number of hours we spend in a day working. It's about the worker.

Time as a tactical and emotional resource

One of my friends jokingly refers to me as a faithful devotee to Our Lady of Perpetual Motion. I run a business, maintain a growing YouTube channel, perform difficult music, write books, maintain a race car, all while being married and raising three teenagers.

Yes, I sleep 8 hours a day and no, I'm not addicted to hustle culture. I treat time management like a skill, because it is. Especially for business owners.

I don't spend all my time reacting to my circumstances. "Busy" is not the same as "effective," so most days I'm building the muscle of intentional time use. For me, time is a competitive advantage instead of a tool. Time used well doesn't lead to burnout. Time spent churning does.

I leave space to think, waiting for ideas to settle before I act. I say yes to the best opportunities available. When I waste time (and I do), I try to make it pay off by mining it for inspiration or clarity. When something's repeatable, I systemize it, automate it, or ask someone smarter how they do it faster.

This is how I get more done and feel better while doing it.

This is what entrepreneurs miss: time is both a tactical resource and an emotional one. How you manage it will shape the kind of life and business you end up with.

AI is coming for your excuses

The TV show Severance imagines a world where people can have a chip implanted in their brains to separate their work memories from their personal ones. It splits a person in two: one version exists only at work, the other only outside of it. Neither knows what the other does all day.

It's a brilliant, unsettling look at the drudgery of modern work and how far people might go to avoid experiencing it.

When the show hit in 2022, OpenAI's ChatGPT was also making headlines. Suddenly, millions of people were asking: "Is this thing going to replace my job?" In mere seconds, AI was writing content, drafting code, building pitch decks, analyzing data. Scary.

And here's the contradiction: a lot of people hate their jobs. They dread Mondays and live for weekends. But the moment a machine shows up offering to take over that job? They panic. We've built an economy on work we don't enjoy, and now we're scared of losing it.

There's a clear entrepreneurial reality: **if you're not using AI to do the parts of your job you don't want to do, someone else is.** Someone faster, cheaper, and more focused. They're spending less time grinding and more time thinking and executing.

AI won't replace all our work, but it will replace people who refuse to evolve. If you're clinging to outdated workflows, doing everything manually, or pretending AI doesn't apply to your industry, you're delaying the inevitable.

You don't need a chip in your brain, but if you ignore the tools that could free you, you're choosing a prison.

It's okay to take time off

STARTUPS FAIL BECAUSE OF FOUNDER BURNOUT

NOT BECAUSE THE FOUNDER TOOK A COUPLE DAYS OFF

Used with permission. © Ash Lamb, ashlamb.com

Time is of the essence

For entrepreneurs, time is more important than money. It's the difference between sanity and wanting to jump off a proverbial bridge. How you spend your time determines whether you stay focused or slide back into the mental prison.

When I managed my time well, I felt capable and clear. When I didn't, I felt stuck, as if everything was decaying around me. I needed more than productivity. I needed momentum because without it, I'd start to spiral out of control.

Burnout doesn't need to come from overwork. In my experience it usually comes from time mismanagement, like when I'm working hard on the wrong things, chasing metrics that don't matter, and doing everything myself because it feels faster than delegating. Plus all that context switching.

It's a predictable pattern for creatives and solopreneurs:

• They gain traction while working full-time

• They quit their jobs to go all-in

• They ride a wave of growth and attention until momentum slows

• They start making decisions based on likes, comments, and imaginary expectations

• They burn out

What started as joy becomes pressure. The hobby becomes a jobby, then a side hustle, and then a survival job. Suddenly, they're not running a business and they're running on fumes.

Productivity is important, but it only gets you so far. Good time management protects your energy, your focus, and your freedom.

Work/Life balance is a made-up thing

There's a "right" number of hours to sleep (roughly 6 to 8), but there's no universal "right" number of hours to work. Some people thrive on 10-hour days, seven days a week. Others cap out at four focused hours, four days a week. Productivity isn't standardized, nor should it be.

Entrepreneurs especially fall into the trap of trying to "optimize" the perfect balance between work and life, as if it's a math problem waiting to be solved. It's not. That's why we work 19 days a week.

Work/life balance is a myth. It sounds good and feels virtuous, but it's built on the false assumption that your energy, attention, and output can be budgeted like money. As if an hour of rest cancels out an hour of work or that your brain runs on some kind of tidy equation.

It doesn't. You're not a spreadsheet.

When entrepreneurs say "work/life balance," what they usually mean is they don't feel in control of their time. They're overwhelmed. They're burned out. They're angry at how they're spending their days, but haven't done the work to change it.

That's not a balance problem. That's a boundaries problem. The better question isn't "How do I balance it all?" It's:

- "Who's in charge of my time?"
- "Who's deciding how I spend my energy?"
- "And does that line up with what I say I value?"

If you're not in charge of those answers, someone else is. That ain't balance, bruv. That's a mental prison.

MENTAL PRISONS

Exposure makes all the difference

According to Jim Rohn, the world-famous motivational speaker and entrepreneur, "You are the average of the five people you spend the most time with."

You might remember the guy pictured on this page as the "friend" who says, "But you're not in prison. Just turn around." It's important that we surround ourselves with people who can tell us the truth. Even better when they can inspire us to be better versions of ourselves.

I spent over 8 years in an entrepreneur support group, developing incredible, life-changing friendships. When we first met, we were all executives working for other people. Now we are all executives running our own companies and have 7-figure net worths. I am absolutely convinced I never would have achieved this without my support group.

If you don't have a support group (or a mentor), I cannot encourage you enough to join (or start) one. Today, they're often called "mastermind groups," but that's usually just a way for business coaches to make money. No matter which way you go, nothing will help you more than exposure to successful people who also want you to succeed.

How success nearly broke me

One of the worst burnout periods of my career hit in 2018. I was working at a 120-person startup that got unexpectedly acquired for $525 million. At first, it was thrilling. Big checks, promotions, raises... the kind of life-changing moment people dream about.

Then came the workload. Yikes. I can already feel my PTSD kicking in.

I helped hire and onboard 90 people in 12 months while simultaneously launching an ambitious new product. The expectations were sky-high, and so were the resources. On paper, it was everything I'd ever wanted, including a nationwide television ad campaign and billboards featuring the product my team was building.

In reality, I was drowning. I worked insane hours, flying back and forth to Chicago constantly, and stretched myself across too many teams and relationships. The joy evaporated. I was exhausted and emotionally frayed. A therapist told me, "If you take a two-week break now, you won't need a six-month one later." I laughed. I didn't have two weeks. (But at least I had free therapy thanks to the Employee Assistance Program!)

The job wasn't bad. I didn't hate the work. But I couldn't do it anymore. Every day was a fog of headaches and dread. I didn't feel alive. I was reacting, trying to keep up while trying not to fall apart.

I can feel the same pit in my stomach I did all those years ago. Every day, I told myself I was lucky to have these circumstances. I was living the startup dream and secretly hating it. 1 star. DO NOT RECOMMEND.

MONDAYS: MAIN IDEAS

☞ "Do I look like someone who would waste his own time?"

☞ Set aside a day of the week to do nothing productive. If it's on a to-do list, don't do it.

☞ Time management is the difference between survival and burning out in a mental prison.

☞ Work/Life balance is a mental prison.

☞ If your business feels like a soul-sucking job, you're doing it wrong. Many entrepreneurs recreate the same misery they escaped from.

Mental Prisons gut check

One of my favorite moments from The Office is during an office manager job interview with a character named Robert California (played by the inimitable James Spader). The interviewer says, "I'm almost a little concerned that you might be overqualified for this position. Do you think you are?" Robert laughs and coldly replies, "Do I look like someone who'd waste my own time?" Which raised some good questions for me:

- What activities do I believe are "wastes of time?" Why?
- What activities are not wastes of time? Why?
- How many of these activities do I participate in every day?
- Do my reasons come down to feelings? Or do I use some form of criteria for evaluating what's a waste of time?
- If I were on a desert island with everything I needed, would I be doing these same behaviors?
- If I tracked all my activities every 15 minutes, would I be proud of how I spend my time? Why or why not?
- How have I spent my time over the past week? Two weeks? Month? Quarter? Half-year? Year?
- Are my activities leading me anywhere? If so, do I like that direction? Why or why not?
- If I could spend a day doing only what served me (and the people who depend on me), what would that look like? What would I cut out and what would I add?
- Do I invest in myself or my future? Are my daily activities part of that investment?
- Are my activities driven by my beliefs or by my DNA? Am I compelled to do these things or am I doing them for "a reason?"
- Do I ever rest? Is resting an activity?

Peter Gibbons:
Let me ask you something. When you come in on Monday, and you're not feelin' real well, does anyone ever say to you, 'Sounds like someone has a case of the Mondays'?

Lawrence:
No. No, man. Sh*t, no, man. I believe you'd get your ass kicked sayin' something like that, man.

– Office Space

CHAPTER SIX

THE DEVIL

THE DEVIL

MENTAL PRISONS

The greatest trick the devil ever pulled was convincing the world he didn't exist.

– Keyser Söze,
The Usual Suspects

Business is spiritual warfare

THE DEVIL

This book isn't here to convince you whether the devil is real. We can't deny the existence of evil nor that there are forces against which we must prevail. As entrepreneurs, we can trivialize it as "it's me versus the world" or we can go as far as to believe that we are in a spiritual fight against a world that doesn't want us to stand up and do our own thing.

I just call this negative force "the devil." Where there's evil and negativity, the devil is found close by.

One of my favorite philosophers, Robert Barron, often says, "Evil is parasitic upon the good." He likens good and evil to a tooth and tooth decay:

> *The tooth is always greater than the cavity. If the cavity totally overwhelms the tooth, you're not talking about a cavity anymore. The tooth is just gone. Now you might talk about, "Oh, well that's bad because there should be a tooth there." [...] And that's why the temptation toward a complete cynicism is metaphysically incoherent. You have to begin and end with the good.*

To run a successful business requires that we believe our business is good. Not just "good" like "nice," but "a force for good in a world that need it." This not only establishes a purpose, but gives us a reason to fight for its existence and for our own freedom.

Having an enemy (even if it's simply a "spiritual" enemy) is important. A business doesn't exist just for the sake of existing. Rather, it exists to bring good into the world, employing and paying people to carry out that mission. And entrepreneurs are the torchbearers bringing light to a dark world.

Free people cannot be controlled

The devil doesn't want us to be free. He doesn't want your business to thrive, and he definitely doesn't want you to feel good about yourself.

Because when you're free, you're dangerous. You can make clear decisions. You're self-directed and can't be controlled. You become unpredictable and open to doing something great.

Even though he represents captivity, the devil always offers a choice. In The Emperor's New Groove, the shoulder devil brags, "He's gonna lead you down the path of righteousness. I'm gonna lead you down the path that rocks."

He reels you in with the short-term hit. The choice that "feels good right now." For instance, in my mental prison, calling myself an idiot felt good. It satisfied the urge to do something, even if that something made things worse. It gave me a little taste of that victim's mindset, which feels so good to so many.

But I've learned I'm not actually an idiot. Sounds crazy, right? Also, I'm not a failure. Knowing that truth makes it way harder to believe the devil's voice.

Sometimes he still whispers, but my free self shows up and says: "Oh, come on. Not that again. You know that's not true." Then I get back to my day.

"Better" actually makes things worse

The Devil wants you to believe that you and your business aren't "good enough." He pushes words like better, improving, growing, and strengthening, which sound helpful but are rooted in comparison.

That's why we have the saying "comparison is the thief of joy." It's about comparing yourself to others and comparing who you are today to your past self.

Typical self-help advice says, "Don't compare yourself to others! Compare yourself to who you were a year ago." But that's still playing the comparison game. It's judging a constantly-moving target that keeps you trapped in performance mode, always chasing some future version of yourself you think is more acceptable.

The worst part? Better feels harmless and like a virtue. But once you believe growth is required to justify your worth, you can never rest. Now you're trying to grow constantly. Forever. Or else you're a failure.

It's subtle and sly. It's still a prison.

What a pain in the arse.

I really hate this whole "growth at all costs" mindset. It's wrong, pervasive, and so many people fall for it.

The devil has more patience than you

You might be tempted to think the devil operates on our human timelines. Unfortunately, that's not how he works. He's not bound by our clock-watching habits or quarterly review cycles. He can wait 10 years, 20 years, or even longer if that's what it takes. Heck, he can even work through your employees, business partners, customers, friends, or family.

He's got nothing else to do, so he waits. As soon as you encounter a speed bump in your business—client churn, revenue drops, pipeline stagnation, product failures, upset customers—he's got leverage.

The moment you're vulnerable, you're an easy target. He whispers doubts into your ear, making you question your decisions and second-guess yourself. He makes it harder to recover from failure by making each subsequent mistake feel like an insurmountable obstacle. He'll make you question your options and then regret your decisions.

He's crafty! **But here's the thing: the devil is no rush to take you down.** He can wait until your business is on autopilot, until you've become complacent and confident. When that happens, he'll strike with everything he's got.

I can't tell you how many times I've been tempted to shut down my business. Not that I ever want to shut down my business, but when things get tough, I start asking myself, "Why am I putting myself through this?"

My friend Allen Plunkett gave me a great counter-approach: set concrete dates for concrete goals. For example: "If I don't pick up two new clients by the end of April, I will stop doing XYZ." The devil hates specificity.

MENTAL PRISONS

It's all about the journey, right?

THE DEVIL

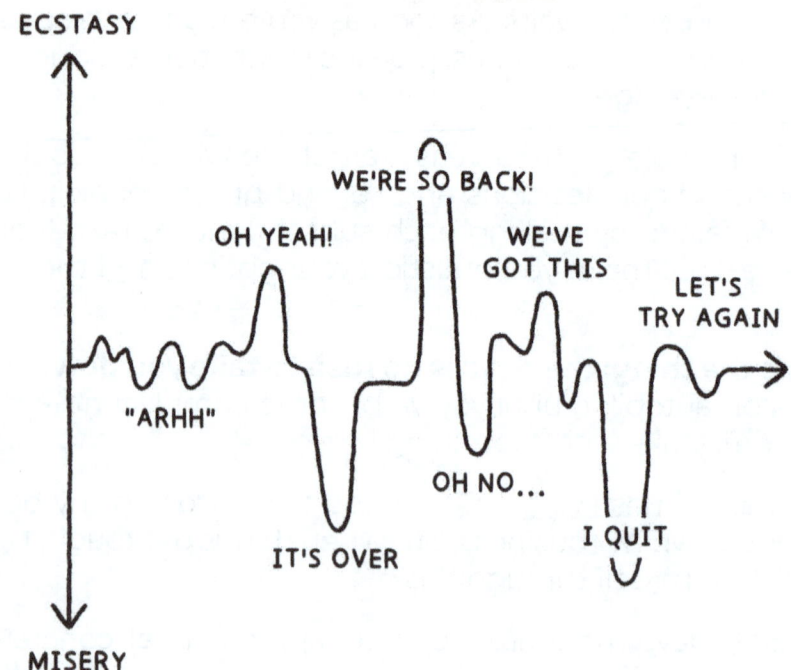

Used with permission. © Ash Lamb, ashlamb.com

The devil has many prisons

THE DEVIL

'Tomorrow' is the first lie of the devil.

– Robert Fripp

The tools of the devil

The devil doesn't need fire and brimstone. He's got way better tools than that: self-doubt, shame, perfectionism, overthinking, procrastination dressed up as "research," fear being disguised as "being realistic," and demoralization. He is far more creative than you might give him credit.

His best trick (and my personal favorite) is convincing you he doesn't exist. That voice in your head saying "You're not ready," "You don't deserve this," "You're going to blow it" It doesn't sound as evil as it sounds familiar and reasonable. That's good marketing.

The devil shows up in your business when you don't raise your prices because you're scared people will leave. You don't launch because the landing page isn't perfect. You take on bad-fit clients because you don't trust there will be better ones. Dumb.

He doesn't come with horns and a pitchfork, either. He shows up as "just how I am." If you don't call him out, you'll start building your business around his advice.

So name the voice and disarm the message. The devil thrives in your compliance. Change the game.

MENTAL PRISONS

THE DEVIL

THE DEVIL: MAIN IDEAS

☞ Evil is parasitic on the good; the better your business, the more resistance you'll face.

☞ Running a business is spiritual warfare. You must believe your business is a force for good.

☞ The devil (metaphorically) wants your business to fail by keeping you in fear, doubt, and self-sabotage.

☞ Freedom in business requires vigilance against internal and external negativity.

☞ Your belief in the mission is your shield against cynicism and burnout.

Mental prison gut check

The devil doesn't show up with horns and fire. He whispers through shame, perfectionism, insecurity, and delay. He doesn't need to destroy you. He just provides enough distraction to keep your focus off the things that matter.

Ask yourself:

- Where am I listening to lies and calling them truth?
- What am I saying to myself that I'd never say to someone I love?
- Am I chasing "better" at the expense of what's already good?
- Who benefits from me believing I'm not good enough?
- What thought patterns feel familiar… but false?
- Where am I calling fear "humility"?
- Am I seeking evidence of my failure or my progress?
- When did I last call myself an idiot? (And why?)
- What flavor of turd sandwich am I still chewing on?
- Is this voice in my head a wise goat… or a snake in disguise?

Remember: the devil's favorite tool is your own voice turned against you.

CHAPTER SEVEN

TURD SANDWICHES

Don't eat turd sandwiches

It sounds like the easiest advice in the world: "Don't eat turd sandwiches." And yet, it's advice I am constantly doling out to myself, my kids, and others, largely because the devil works through other people.

Sometimes he doesn't show up in your head, but in someone else's mouth. If he can't get you to believe your business was a huge mistake, he'll find someone else to say it out loud for him. That's a turd sandwich.

I used to eat a lot of them. "I'm lazy." "I'm difficult." "I'm not leadership material." Every time I accepted one of those labels, I took a bite. Over time, I acquired a taste for them.

Now? If someone hands me a turd sandwich, I leave. Not because I'm cruel or don't care, but because I know a mental prison when I see one. I'm not interested in picking up those bars just because someone else hasn't figured out how to put theirs down.

In the excellent book Crucial Conversations, this same dynamic is called the fool's choice: believing there are only two options (both bad) when there's usually a third, better one.

You don't have to argue or prove anyone wrong. Just don't eat the sandwich.

Turd sandwich menu

Turd of Obligation: "If you want to earn your paycheck, do this for me."

Turd of Reciprocation: "Remember when I helped you with that client?"

Turd of Envy: "But you have more XYZ than I do."

Turd of Aimless Frustration: "I just need to unload this on someone."

Turd of Genetic Loyalty: "You were born into this family. This is how we do things."

Turd of Superiority: "I'm busy with real work. Can you handle the small stuff?"

Turd of Guilt: "Wow. Must be nice to have boundaries."

Turd of Martyrdom: "Don't worry about me. I'll just do everything myself."

Turd of Victimhood: "You wouldn't understand. You've had it easier."

Turd of Manipulated Logic: "Well if you really cared, you'd already know what to do."

Turd of Reputation Leverage: "I told everyone you were reliable. Don't make me look bad!"

Turd of Emotional Blackmail: "I guess I just mean less to you than your work."

Turd of Passive-Aggression: "Sure, no problem. You do you." (Translated: you've just ruined everything.)

The three most harmful addictions are heroin, carbohydrates, and a monthly salary.

– Nassim Nicholas Taleb

There's no science to business

There's a big difference between science and "scientism"—the misguided belief that everything worth knowing can be measured, tested, and peer-reviewed.

I cannot begin to explain how dumb and wrong this is.

Science is useful for explaining the physical world. It won't help you figure out how to price your offer, fire a bad client, or get unstuck after six months of zero momentum.

Still, people love to talk about "the science of success" or "data-driven leadership" like they're guaranteed paths to a thriving business. They're not. That's just professional-grade BS.

Running a business is messy and emotional. As Michael Scott said in The Office, "Business is the most personal thing in the world." Running a business requires taste, timing, risk, creativity, and gut instinct. Those aren't quantifiable.

Thousands of online BS vendors want to sell you "the perfect formula." If you follow their framework, use the right metrics, and copy the habits of top performers, you'll get the same outcome. That ain't it. You're building something that's never existed before. How can their fortune-cookie, one-size-fits-all advice work in the first place?

You can't spreadsheet your way to insight. And you definitely can't automate your own instincts.

Burnout is a turd sandwich

Burnout is never a dramatic collapse, but a slow, sneaky snuffing out of an inner flame. It's also a turd sandwich. The first bite has an "I'm so tired" flavor. The second tastes like "I'm in a brain fog." The third bite is really heavy and dense, like a flourless chocolate cake—but, you know, poop.

We keep chewing because we think we have to. "This is just the price of growing a business." It's a trap.

You stop noticing how disgusting everything tastes because you've normalized eating a turd sandwich.

When I was at my worst with burnout, I wrote this down on a post-it note:

Inside of you is a fire.

Protect it.

Do not let it burn out.

Even if it is the tiniest flame,

It is precious.

It is all you have.

There's no "powering through it" or "getting over the slump." You're eating a turd sandwich and you need to stop. Reading that note did it for me. Find something that does it for you.

Are you eating turd sandwiches?

Here's a series of questions I used to determine whether I was eating turd sandwiches and what I could do about it.

- What's the last turd sandwich I recall eating? When and why did I do it?
- Did I have any other choices than to eat it? If I said "no," what's the worst that could have happened?
- Am I eating them out of a lack of self-respect? Do I believe myself to be a martyr? Is the other person too "important" or "significant" to deny?
- Would I rather feel bad and eat it, or feel "good" but face consequences?
- Am I enabling the sandwich-offering by saying "yes" on a regular basis?
- What is the reputational cost for saying "no" to these sandwiches? Is there anything at stake for me?
- Could I have done anything beforehand to have prevented being handed the sandwich?
- Do I enjoy the taste of turds? Do I enjoy suffering?
- What are the precursors I could (or should) have identified before I was offered the sandwich?
- Is it better to avoid the sandwich altogether or to say "no" when offered to eat it?
- In an ideal world, how should I respond when I am offered a bite?

TURD SANDWICHES: MAIN IDEAS

☞ Every business has hard, messy parts. What you're willing to tolerate defines your entrepreneurial path.

☞ Success requires deciding which "turd sandwich" you're willing to eat; you can't avoid eating one.

☞ You'll never find a perfect opportunity, only a set of tradeoffs you're willing to live with.

☞ Delaying decisions or seeking perfect conditions is just another form of mental prison.

Mental prison gut check

Not all feedback is helpful. Not all expectations are fair. Some are hot garbage wrapped in obligation and guilt.

Ask yourself:

- Am I tolerating someone else's dysfunction because I feel I "should"?
- Who's handing me turd sandwiches and why do I keep taking bites?
- Do I confuse being agreeable with being responsible?
- What's the cost of saying yes when I mean no?
- Am I carrying emotional debt from favors I didn't ask for?
- When was the last time I accepted guilt as a valid form of payment?
- Does this relationship feel like connection… or control?
- What do I owe, really and what have I just been guilted into?
- Is this advice helpful or a projection of someone else's ideas/needs?
- What would happen if I put the sandwich down and walked away?

Spoiler: the people who love you don't serve you crap on a paper plate and expect a thank-you.

*Everything can be seen directly
except the eye through which we see.
Every thought can be scrutinized directly
except the thought by which we scrutinize.*

– E. F. Schumacher, A Guide for the Perplexed

CHAPTER EIGHT

THE ENEMY

Meet your co-founder: self-sabotage

Every time I ghost a warm lead, procrastinate on an important pitch, overthink a simple project, or avoid a tough conversation, it's not because I'm "too busy" or "being strategic."

It's self-sabotage.

I've blamed clients, market timing, competition, and even algorithms. But the truth is, the call is coming from inside the house.

Self-sabotage is sneaky. It wears disguises like perfectionism, overplanning, burnout, or being "realistic." It's the part of me that would rather fail on my own terms than succeed in a way I don't fully control. It's the part that's scared of visibility, risk, vulnerability, or success itself.

And it's a hell of a co-founder.

The worst part? Self-sabotage doesn't always tank the business. Sometimes it lets you win just enough to avoid scrutiny. You hit your numbers. You make progress. But deep down, you know you're playing small. You're building around fear, not vision.

That voice in your head saying "Don't send it. Don't ask. Don't launch. Don't try."

That's your co-founder talking. Time to fire them.

Positivity sucks

Entrepreneurs are told to "stay positive," especially when things suck. But we don't give in to tyranny, do we?! Hah! Forget forced optimism with fakey statements like "Just stay positive." "Mindset is everything." "Good vibes only." It's that kind of thinking that turns business owners into pressure cookers.

I'm with Dr. Susan David, who tweeted: "Normal, natural emotions are often seen as good or bad, and being positive has become a new form of moral correctness. It's a tyranny of positivity."

When things go sideways (and you know they will), who do you talk to if you're not allowed to sound negative? Who helps you when your default is "It's fine, everything's fine"?

Negativity isn't the problem. Avoiding it is.

I don't want to wallow in pessimism, but I also don't want to duct-tape a smile onto something that's not working. If I can't be honest about what's hard—cash flow, burnout, bad hires, self-doubt—then I can't fix it.

Positivity, when forced, becomes delusion. And delusion kills businesses. Entrepreneurs don't need fake cheer. We need clarity. We need space to say, "This is hard," without fear that we're going to be steamrolled by positivity chuds.

We need to feel the lows so we can move through them and not get stuck pretending everything is up and to the right.

So no, I'm not chasing positivity. I'm chasing truth. When I'm grounded in reality, I make better decisions and I build something worth showing up for.

Perfectionism

I used to roll my eyes at the word "perfectionist." That's not me, I thought. I'm just detail-oriented, responsible, and thorough. Turns out: that's exactly what perfectionists tell themselves.

Dr. Paul Hewitt studies perfectionism at the University of British Columbia. He writes:

> Two particularly intriguing paradoxes with perfectionism have captured our attention and have dominated our thinking over the past several years. First, why does perfectionism persist, given its costs? [...] The second paradox reflects the theme introduced earlier: Perfectionism, at its core, is rooted in the relational world of the individual. It also reflects that perfectionism is the result of one of the most basic motivated forces among humans: the need to attain a sense of felt security and self-regard through being accepted, respected, and cared for, and mattering to others—in essence a sense of belonging.

That sure sounds like the core problem of mental prisons: you're trying to earn love and belonging through impossibly-high performance expectations. More interesting commentary on the people who suffer from perfectionism:

> Some of these individuals can be quite accomplished and successful according to objective criteria, but **it often seems as if their achievements are secrets that have been kept from them**. That is, they have lived their lives and evaluated themselves by expectations, either their own or others', that are impossible to meet.

And an interesting question from Hewitt: "Why not strive for excellence rather than absolute perfection?"

There's no such thing as a perfect business, but perfectionists keep chasing one at the expense of actual progress. If we aim for perfect, we can achieve excellence.

Discover your business, don't invent it

Musician Trey Gunn once told me that musicians are like mathematicians and archaeologists. Mathematicians don't invent the laws of the universe. They discover them through experimentation. Similarly, archaeologists don't invent the past. They uncover it by digging and exploring.

The same is true for business. I've found substantial relief in knowing I don't need to invent the next big thing. My company and its services are relatively boring, so I don't have to be a visionary genius. It's one less thing I have to think about. Most of the time, I just need to be sensitive enough to my circumstances that I can sniff out opportunities.

Running a business doesn't require conjuring brilliance out of thin air. However, it does require paying attention, listening, testing, tinkering, and digging. All I have to do is discover what already works, what customers already want, what people are already struggling with, then align my products and services with those realities.

I don't need to reinvent the wheel. I just need to find one that's rolling and figure out how to make it roll better, faster, or in a new direction.

When we stop trying to invent the future, we create space to discover what's already true and build something real on top of it.

Then make money. Right?

As our island of knowledge grows, so does the shore of our ignorance.

— John Wheeler

The more I know, the less I know

Anonymous Twitter/X account @AlsekDreams wrote: "Clarity of vision does not increase with the quantity of information you consume." Ain't that the truth.

I've worked and lived with an unfair number of geniuses. Believe me, when I say "genius," I mean it in the most serious definition of the word. I'm talking about people who are internationally recognized as certified smartypants, having changed their professional fields through innovative work and experimentation. These are people who are revered by other geniuses.

For example, I worked for Danny Hillis, who invented massively parallel processing back in the 1980s, worked with Richard Feynman, built a clock that will run for 10,000 years on gravity alone, and helped Jeff Bezos start Amazon.com. Danny was on vacation in Hawaii and Steve Jobs, who happened to be there at the same time, approached Danny to have a conversation. Yeah.

I've also worked and lived with an unfair number of armchair experts. You know, the types of people who will spend an entire afternoon happily telling me how to lose weight and what "calories in, calories out" means, all while having a belly hang over their pants.

Both armchair experts and legitimate geniuses spend a lot of time learning and consuming information. However, real-world geniuses consume information strategically, for a greater purpose so that they can apply it. Armchair experts consume information competitively to feel greater than others.

I've consumed a lot of information and wasted a lot of time pretending knowledge was the same thing as progress. The more I learn, the more I realize how little I understand. The deeper I go, the more I appreciate clarity over volume.

When it comes to running a business, knowledge is useful, but clarity is power.

Informing ourselves to death

This page contains a block of text that was too long for one of those colored quote pages, so I'm allocating a normal-looking page for it here. In a speech to the German Informatics Society in 1990, Neil Postman said:

> *If children die of starvation in Ethiopia, does it occur because of a lack of information? If criminals roam the streets of New York City, do they do so because of a lack of information? If you and your spouse are unhappy together, and end your marriage in divorce, will it happen because of a lack of information? [...]*
>
> *I believe you will have to concede that what ails us, what causes us the most misery and pain—at both cultural and personal levels—has nothing to do with the sort of information made accessible by computers. The computer and its information cannot answer any of the fundamental questions we need to address to make our lives more meaningful and humane. The computer cannot provide an organizing moral framework. It cannot tell us what questions are worth asking.*

This is a great excerpt to read when I need a reminder that I'm spending too much time online. Learning is good, but there comes a point at which "learning" isn't much more than consuming information.

As we enter the age of artificial intelligence, may we keep Neil's words close to our hearts.

Yes, you will have enemies (competition)

This book is largely focused on the enemy within, but let's be real: there are definitely enemies outside your head. Sometimes they're your direct competitors, other times they're strangers on the internet. They could also be people who, for whatever reason, don't like you, your business, your products or services, or even the fact that you're doing your own thing. They might even dislike you because you are succeeding or because they're envious of your progress.

Heck, I know from personal experience that:

1. People dislike me

2. I dislike other people.

3. Sometimes my own dislike shows up as envy.

Despite all my personal progress and hard work, I often catch myself comparing. I see someone post a huge revenue month and immediately think, "What am I doing wrong?" even if I just had a great month myself. That's one of my personal mental prisons, and I'm still working through it.

But here's what I've learned: enemies—real or perceived—aren't the problem. My reaction is. If I let envy or resentment take over, it slows me down, muddying my judgment, making me forget why I started a business in the first place.

Competition is inevitable. So is criticism. Let them exist. Let them motivate you if they must, but don't let them rent space in your head.

We've got better things to build.

Let Wisdom quietly guide your business

The devil wants us to fail and has an uncanny knack for whispering believable lies into our ears. But there's another voice inside us: the goat.

The goat is the part of us that knows better.

He's not as loud as the devil. He doesn't beg for attention. He shows up with quiet clarity and says, "You don't need to do that. You know this isn't true. You've already done harder things than this."

The goat doesn't offer new insight. He just reminds us of what we already know.

Most of the time, I don't need more information. I don't need another framework. I've read all the books, listened to all the podcasts, watched all the TED talks.

In moments of difficulty, I need to pursue what is good and true, avoiding the temptation to pick up the bars of my mental prison.

The goat doesn't pull the bars out of your hands. He simply tells you to loosen your fingers and let go.

Do you need any more than that?

MENTAL PRISONS

THE ENEMY

*Watching someone else
totally go for it
can be incredibly upsetting
to the person who has
spent a lifetime
building a solid case
for why they themselves can't.*

– Jen Sincero

☞ Your biggest enemy is often internal: your voice of doubt, fear, and perfectionism.

☞ We tell ourselves damaging stories about who we are and what we're capable of.

☞ External enemies (critics, competitors) are rarely as harsh as our inner critic.

☞ Knowing yourself clearly (your values, your strengths) is key to defeating the enemy within.

Mental prison gut check

Do you really think you know who you are? I'm 90% sure you don't, and that's not just because this is a book called Mental Prisons. Most of the time, the people I talk to don't know how good they are, how and why they are revered or respected, or even that there are people who look up to them. Here are some questions I ran through to better understand myself.

Fact checking:

- What am I most competent at? In what ways am I an expert?
- Do I often undermine myself? If so, how? What are the behaviors?
- If I asked my friends, how would they answer? (Actually go ask friends. Don't just imagine an answer on their behalf.)
- What are the common themes about me and my expertise based on that feedback?
- Do my friends think I undermine myself? If so, how?

Values::

- What are the top 10 values that drive my professional and personal behaviors?
- CRGLeader.com has an excellent Values Preference Indicator (VPI) assessment, which greatly helped me. They use the following values: Accomplishments, Acknowledgement, Challenge, Cooperation, Creativity, Expertise, Friendship, Honesty, Independence, Instruction, Intimacy, Organization, Pleasure, Quality, Recognition, Responsibility, Security, Spirituality, Tranquility, Variety, Wealth
- Am I living and working in alignment with my values? How so? And why (or why not)?

Most people think they know what they are good at. They are usually wrong. More often, people know what they are not good at— and then even more people are more wrong than right. And yet, a person can only perform from strength.

– Peter Drucker, Managing Oneself

CHAPTER NINE

scarcity

At the heart of business scarcity is a chase

Entrepreneurs are natural chasers. We are always pursuing revenue, logos, visibility, funding, and market share. Those are usually the symptoms of an underlying root cause: we are chasing the feelings we think they'll give us.

When I first started my business, I chased clients that weren't a good fit, projects I didn't care about, and metrics I didn't fully believe in. Why? Because I thought they'd make me look like I was winning. It's a fantasy that's about what you think it says about you.

At one point, I landed a Fortune 500 client that sounded exciting. I had about 30 seconds of dopamine, followed by six months of grind and regret. We couldn't even finish one deliverable because they were so inefficient and bloated. I wasn't set up to work with a client like that and we never got paid because none of us (including the procurement team) could wrap our heads around their invoicing system. I gave up after months of trying until someone sent me a handwritten check.

The mental prison makes you believe that when the chase is over, you'll finally be free. But "chasing" is an addiction that feeds on momentum, not fulfillment. That's why they call it the hedonic treadmill. You run hard and get nowhere.

I think about Aesop's fable of the fox and the sour grapes. The fox wants the grapes, but they're juuuust out of reach, so he convinces himself they were probably sour anyway. That's how the prison justifies the chase. When you get what you want and it doesn't satisfy you, the next goal magically appears.

At some point, you have to ask: Am I building something meaningful or chasing something I hope will "finally" make me feel better?

A business thrives on abundance

It's easy to get caught in the loop: so much to do, so little time. You're slammed with work, moving fast, checking boxes. If someone dares to suggest simplifying, your instinct is to snap: "You think I have time for that?"

Unless you're the first person in human history to encounter this problem, you are wrong.

I've been there. When I'm buried in tasks, the idea of stepping back to reorganize or refocus feels like a luxury you can't afford. Not only that, but it feels like it's impossible. "I know my situation better than anyone else! I know what I'm going through! There's no fix!"

Yeah, right. **If you're so smart, why are you in this situation?**

That "nobody else understands" mindset is a trap. It trains you to run your business from a place of scarcity. You hoard time, chase every opportunity, and say yes to things just because they're in front of you.

Abundance is less about excess and more about alignment. It means building a business that gives you time to think, space to breathe, and clarity about where you're going. Not because everything's perfect, but because you've chosen not to run at redline all day, every day.

Most of the best decisions I've made didn't come from chaos. They came from having room to consider, to listen, to see clearly. And that only happens when you stop treating busyness like a badge of honor.

If you're always too busy to make things better, the business will keep demanding more and more—until you break, or it does.

SCARCITY

"But, I don't have enough time"

Yes, you do!

Run your business on 36-hour days

Stop supporting the time industrial complex. Don't think of hours in 60-minute increments. Think in 40-minute blocks, call that an "hour," and get 12 more hours in your day. This might sound like a joke, but it's not. I literally wrote the javascript to convert time to 36-hour days. Noon is at 18:00. Midnight is at 36:00.

That shift alone changed everything for me. I get more "hours" out of a day. I don't have to work longer if I redefine what an hour is. (Yes, I know how stupid this sounds.)

We cling to round numbers: 9 to 5. Meetings on the hour. Calls starting at :00 or :30. But time isn't naturally round or divisible by 15 minute increments. We made it that way, which means we can unmake it into something just as arbitrary.

As an entrepreneur, time is your most limited and abused resource. You can't scale yourself, but you can shrink the blocks you operate in. You can compress work without sacrificing quality. **A 40-minute work session is often more productive than a 90-minute one filled with Slack pings and tab-switching.**

Over time, your internal clock resets. You stop thinking, "I need an hour to do this," and start thinking, "Can I do this in 40? 25? Can I do it better in less?" Time expands when you treat it like a design problem instead of a rulebook.

So no, I don't have 36 literal hours in my day. I just don't let the clock tell me how to spend mine.

The less I do, the better my business runs

When asked how he sculpted David, Michelangelo supposedly said, "I simply carved away everything that wasn't David." That's the principle of via negativa (progress by removal). Subtraction, not addition.

For most of my life, I operated on via positiva. If something wasn't working, I added more: more projects, more responsibilities, more hobbies, more ways to prove I was doing enough. Because deep down, I didn't believe I was enough.

That mindset doesn't scale, especially when running a business.

Life isn't a salad. I can't keep adding ingredients until it tastes right. I'm managing a complex system: a brain, a body, a family, a business, a future. At some point, more doesn't help. It just weighs me down.

I've learned that doing less doesn't mean being lazy. It means carving away what doesn't belong (tasks, roles, responsibilities, distractions) so what matters can actually work.

I used to feel guilty for not doing everything. Now I feel proud of doing the right things well.

Five things with focus beats ten things with resentment. (Almost) every time.

Conflicting business advice isn't hypocrisy

Entrepreneurs are surrounded by contradictory advice: work harder, rest more; niche down, diversify; raise prices, lower friction; do more, do less; do more with less. It's hard to tell the difference between wisdom and noise. But what looks like contradiction might only be contextual wisdom.

There's an old story about a teacher who had two students, each with the same hand injury. He told one to wash in cold water. The other with warm water.

A confused student asked, "Why the conflicting advice?" The teacher replied, "Both are off the path. One needs to turn left. The other needs to turn right."

As Duncan Watts writes in Everything is Obvious (Once You Know the Answer), common sense is often self-contradictory:

- "Opposites attract," but "birds of a feather flock together."
- "Absence makes the heart grow fonder," but "out of sight, out of mind."
- "Experience is the best teacher," but "keep a beginner's mind."
- It's a mess of aphorisms and most of it is only useful in hindsight.

In business, this shows up everywhere and it's really stupid. One founder's breakthrough came from slowing down. Another's came from going all in. One scaled by saying no. Another grew by saying yes to everything until the signal was obvious. Who cares.

When you're looking for your way out of the mental prison, don't ask which path is "right."

Ask: Which direction gets me back on my path?

Humans focus on the negative

In his book *The Happiness Advantage,* author Shawn Achor points out something wild: For every one study on positivity, there are seventeen on negativity. That's a "17-to-1 negative-to-positive ratio in the entire field of psychology." No wonder we default to focusing on what's broken.

As humans—and especially as entrepreneurs (hey, we're human, right?)—we're wired to scan for threats. If we didn't, we'd get blindsided. You can't build a business while pretending everything's fine. You have to notice the dip in cash flow, the unhappy client, the employee who's about to quit. There's a good reason our brains are tuned to spot danger.

But when you live in a mental prison, that danger-sensing mechanism doesn't shut off. It exaggerates risk and turns every stumble into a sign of inevitable failure. You start to ignore wins entirely. Often, you'll hit your goals and immediately move the goalposts, obsessing over what's missing instead of what's working. ("I finally got to $30K/mo., but that's not enough. I need to hit $50K/mo. and and and.")

Here's the thing: being realistic doesn't require being pessimistic. You can stay grounded without spiraling. You can address problems without thinking you are the problem. That's the difference between rational assessment and prison-thinking.

Noticing what's broken isn't a problem unless it's the only thing you notice.

☞ Scarcity thinking is rooted in fear and leads to endless chasing: more revenue, more recognition, more control.

☞ We often mistake achievement for fulfillment, leading to burnout.

☞ Entrepreneurs struggle to define "enough," which feeds anxiety and endless dissatisfaction.

☞ True freedom comes from shifting away from scarcity toward sufficiency and gratitude.

Mental Prison Gut Check

Scarcity mindset drives us to live like everything's about to disappear, which is totally ridiculous and normal for a mental prisoner. There's much more to scarcity than money and it affects the entirety of our lives, putting undue pressure on us well beyond our work hours.

In turn, we end up having a creeping sense that no matter what we earn, do, or accomplish, it's never quite enough. And then we "reframe" it into "ambition," which is just fear wearing shiny shoes and a nice hat.

Dealing with scarcity means rethinking our relationship with "enough" by asking:

- What's the number in my head that feels safe, legitimate, or "real"?
- Have I already hit numbers I used to think were impossible? Do I feel proud of that?
- What milestone(s) am I chasing that might not actually matter?
- Do I trust that more is coming or do I act like the next customer is the last one?
- Am I building a business or a treadmill that just gets faster and angrier?
- Do I believe success has to feel stressful to count?
- Who taught me this nonsense? And why am I still listening?

Don't fool yourself by reframing scarcity as hustle, realism, or responsibility. If you're always grinding, reaching, and feeling behind, you're just running on fear instead of freedom.

Happiness is not having what you want, but wanting what you have.

– Rabbi Hyman Schachtel

CHAPTER TEN

RESPONSIBILITY

MENTAL PRISONS

"How am I complicit?"

Before we dig into the comic on the previous page, I want to preface these pages with a more elegant and digestible explanation from leadership coach Jerry Colonna on Lenny Rachitsky's May 2025 podcast. It's easy to interpret my comic (which is intentionally provocative) in a way that may be hurtful, or even harmful. Here's how Jerry put it and how we should think about it in this section:

> The question that I often ask is: How have I been complicit in creating the conditions I say I don't want?
>
> I purposely chose the word "complicit" because complicit does not mean "responsible." That's a really important distinction. As I often say: to understand the word "complicit," think of the word "accomplice." You are driving the getaway car. You're not sticking up the bank teller.
>
> The second half of that question is: "I say I don't want." Sometimes people hear that question and they interpret it as: "How have I been responsible for the shit in my life?" And that is not the purpose of this question.
>
> The purpose of this question is actually to evoke your own agency. It's to look at the ways in which you may have been deluding yourself. A perfect example of that would be:
>
> I say I don't want to feel busy all the time. But the truth of the matter is: I feel really unnerved and disconcerted if my agenda isn't jam-packed.
>
> The reason this is all really important is that part of my approach not only to coaching, but the process of growing up, is to use what I call "radical self inquiry" to really cut through our own delusions and say, "How does it serve me to feel completely busy to the point where I feel exhausted?" And perhaps there's a more conscious way of getting that feeling than feeling like crap all the time.

I am responsible for my business

When I posted this chapter's comic strip to Facebook, I got all kinds of grief. One person called me "irresponsible." Another person said,"But this isn't true. I appreciate the sentiment, but it doesn't square with what we know about generational, racial, and economic inequity."

Some of the criticism is perhaps well-deserved, but here's the thing: How can a difficult statement communicate an idea or teach a lesson? How can we learn from a statement that seems harsh and unfair?

Most importantly, why do so many successful entrepreneur friends agree with it? "I am responsible" is a tough pill to swallow, for sure, but those of us who take extreme ownership don't seem to have an issue with it.

When I first encountered this idea of being responsible for "everything," I was taken aback. In fact, I found myself shocked and outraged the more I thought about it. "You are responsible for everything that happens to you." All these whataboutisms came to me, like "what about people who get cancer?"

Over time, however, I realized that "responsibility" is not the same as "fault." I am certainly responsible for how I react to my circumstances, but I am certainly not at fault for my circumstances.

Whether my business thrives or tanks, I am responsible for that. If someone comes in and steals all my money, I am responsible for that.

I may not be at fault for what happens to my business, but I am responsible for what happens next. **If something goes wrong, I have to fix it.**

Extreme business ownership

The concept of "extreme ownership" was popularized by Jocko Willink and Leif Babin, two former U.S. Navy SEAL officers. It centers around taking full responsibility for your results, even when it feels unfair. ("There are no bad teams, only bad leaders.")

You don't wait or depend on anyone else. You decide what you're going to do, then you execute. The upside: you take complete control of everything in your life. The downside: the results are entirely your fault—good or bad. No excuses.

As the owner of a business that sells writing services, ChatGPT and other AI-based services are causing my potential customers to question whether high-quality writing is worth paying for. In late 2023, I lost 80% of my business, largely due to the impact of AI on my market.

I could easily have said, "It's not my fault AI disrupted my services." Instead, I had to admit that my business wasn't resilient enough to withstand the impact of AI. Since then, I've come up with new service offerings and have kept the company going.

Since taking radical ownership over my business, I've made far fewer excuses and work every day to mitigate the risk of failure. While other friends are completely out of work, I'm continuing to generate more than $40K per month for writing services.

Owning my thoughts and feelings, too

Another idea communicated in the previous comic is that you and I are responsible for what we think and how we feel. This is difficult to reconcile, but hard to deny.

As I've told my children many times, "Don't tell me your brother made you angry. Unless he can also make you happy, then he can't make you angry. And from what I can tell, he couldn't make you happy no matter how hard he tries."

You are responsible for everything you think and feel.

I know my thinking can be influenced, but it can't be outright controlled. If someone tells me, "Don't think of an elephant," I'm going to think of an elephant anyway. But if they tell me, "You need to hire so-and-so," I'm not going to sacrifice my overhead and profitability without a very, very good reason.

Similarly, no one can force me to feel something. Though the latest research on emotions shows there are foundational emotional building blocks in our subconscious mind, we still don't really understand how or why emotions work. Yes, we can be manipulated, but it's not so simple that just anyone could do it.

Therefore, I am always free to think any thoughts at any time, whether I'm in a mental prison or not. And no matter my circumstances, my emotions can't be controlled.

The upside of stress

Most entrepreneurs probably think stress is a bad thing, like a physiological tax, a threat to your well-being, or a signal you're doing something wrong. But what if stress is part of what makes you great?

Keith Rabois, an early exec at PayPal, Square, LinkedIn, and now a VC at Founders Fund, believes stress is misunderstood. He recommends The Upside of Stress by Kelly McGonigal, a book that reframes stress as something that can enhance performance, resilience, and even longevity, depending on how you interpret it.

According to Rabois, the problem isn't stress itself but how we react to it. When you treat stress as a challenge rather than a danger, it becomes fuel. Founders often operate in this zone by default. Pressure pushes us to perform. Stress isn't as much a glitch in the system as it is part of the system.

That said, even Rabois knows when stress becomes counterproductive. His company OpenStore exists to relieve stress for entrepreneurs by buying or managing their e-commerce businesses. Stress can push you, but it can also wear you down. Knowing the difference is the practice we need to develop.

You don't need to eliminate stress to be a good founder. But you do need to stop fearing it. Stress can mean something's wrong, or it can mean you're doing something hard that matters. Sometimes it's both.

Either way, just because there's fear in the air doesn't mean it's time to stop. Usually it means it's time to get serious.

Who controls my business, anyway?

Business owners sure do love talking and thinking about freedom: the freedom to choose our work, build our vision, set our own hours, be our own boss, and even work from anywhere in the world where there's an internet connection.

But when things get tough, a strange thing happens: we start handing over control.

We blame the market. We blame flaky customers. We blame lazy employees, bad leads, aggressive competitors, the algorithm, or "the economy." And sure, those things matter. But they don't run your business. You do.

Every time you say "I can't because..." and point outward, you reinforce a story where you're not the one driving. You start living reactively. Waiting. Hoping. Justifying.

That's not freedom. That's a cage with an ergonomic desk chair.

You can't control your customers, the economy, or whether someone ghosts your proposal. But you can control your response. Your strategy. Your priorities. Your time.

If you started a business to be in charge, act like it. If you don't run your business, someone else will—probably by accident. Here are some questions to ask:

- Am I the CEO of my company, or an employee with a bad boss?
- Am I leading a company to success or reacting to whatever comes my way?
- Do I secretly resent my customers, clients/partners, team, and/or industry?
- Who is responsible for my stress right now?
- What's one thing I keep blaming on "the market" that I haven't actually tried to solve?

I am okay with my mental prison

Mental performance coach Kapil Gupta has been one of the biggest inspirations in my journey to mental freedom. He said:

"The only reason that you don't have what you want is because you did not really want it. The only reason you have the things that you do is because you couldn't live without them. And the only reason that you are where you are is because somewhere within you it is okay to be there."

When I reflect on time served in my mental prison, I realize that I've never been so bothered by it as to change. If I start looking fat, I eat less and work out more. If I feel like my guitar chops are fading, I practice more. If my revenue goes down, I do more cold outreach and networking.

Some situations are acceptable, others are not. Having spent 30 years in a mental prison, it's obvious that the mental prison was acceptable to me. I could tolerate it and still get on with my life.

Which leads me to realize: the only reason I'm ever in prison is because I'm okay with it. The reason I'm overweight is because I'm fine carrying around an extra 10-15 pounds. I'm okay swearing on occasion. I'm okay smelling bad at times. I'm okay going to bed without brushing my teeth.

It happens because I tolerate it. What else do I tolerate?

- What's one habit I complain about but secretly accept?
- What belief about myself have I never seriously challenged?
- Where in my life do I settle because it's easier than changing?
- What am I avoiding that would probably improve my life?

☞ Blaming others (the market, your clients, your team) is giving away your power.

☞ Mental freedom begins when you own every decision—even the bad ones.

☞ If you started a business to be in charge, you need to act like it.

☞ Radical responsibility brings clarity, direction, and energy back into your business.

Mental prison gut check

Responsibility is easy to talk about when things are going well. But when revenue drops, a client leaves, or a product flops, it's tempting to shift the blame. "The market changed." "That employee dropped the ball." "Nobody told me." These are comforting lies that strip us of agency. As entrepreneurs, we don't always control the outcomes, but we do control our actions, decisions, and mindset.

Ask yourself:

- When something goes wrong, do I look for root causes or someone to blame?
- Am I blaming the market, my team, or my customers... instead of my decisions?
- Do I believe I control my calendar or does everyone else?
- When I say "I don't have time," is that actually true?
- Have I made a clear decision or am I waiting for someone else to make it for me?
- Do I avoid certain tasks because I resent being the one responsible for them?
- Am I acting like the CEO or just playing one in Slack?
- What would change if I took radical ownership of my business and life?
- Who's really running this business: me, or my excuses?

Responsibility isn't a punishment. Own it or someone else will.

When we become responsible for our own values, we no longer have to struggle to make the world conform to our needs. Rather we adapt our own values to fit the circumstances that confront us in the world.

– William James

CHAPTER ELEVEN

READINESS

MENTAL PRISONS

READINESS

Letting go of the habit of hanging on

There's always resistance when you try to leave your mental prison. Sometimes it's internal thoughts focused on doubt, fear, and inertia.

Sometimes it sounds like a voice in your head saying, "Come on, you've held onto those bars your whole life. Why stop now?"

That voice is lying. But, gotdang, it's persuasive and reveals a hard truth: **holding on to the bars is the habit.**

You don't have to "try" to grip the bars because you do it by default. Letting go, on the other hand, is unfamiliar. It takes intention. When you try to let go of a belief or behavior that's been with you for so long, it feels like letting go of you.

For me, it came down to one hard question: Do I want to live the rest of my life feeling this way?

I had this feeling like I'm not as good as I am and I need to suffer to grow. Ugh, it makes me sick, like I'm a "problem" to be "fixed." I saw a therapist, read the books, and knew what to do. Still, I did nothing to fix it.

Whether I had a victim's mindset doesn't matter. I was giving too much power to my circumstances and emotions, acting like my story wasn't mine to rewrite.

At some point, I started realizing my life is a place of high adventure. I can decide whether I keep carrying the bars or set them down. That's cool!

But first, I had to admit: I've been the one holding them.

It's not ok to be not ok

There's a (dumb) popular message floating around: "It's okay not to be okay." I get that it's meant to be comforting and reduce stigma, but I hate it.

Here's the problem: "It's okay not to be okay" sounds compassionate, but for many entrepreneurs, it becomes a permission slip for emotional complacency. It turns survival mode into a lifestyle. It suggests that your current brokenness is somehow sustainable. It isn't.

This is not a job where you get to float. Founders don't have the luxury of spiraling forever. If your business is flailing, your mind is a mess, and your inbox is an avalanche, no amount of "not okay" is going to help you lead. Your team doesn't need your trauma, but they they do need your presence.

It's not okay to normalize burnout or to fake confidence when you're collapsing. And it's definitely not okay to keep pretending things will magically get better if you never take action.

Yes, we all fall apart sometimes. But part of being a grown-up (especially one who signs the checks) is learning how to catch yourself, ask for help, and get back up.

You can't run a business if you're "not ok." So ditch the silly pop culture message and replace it with, "This isn't working, and I need to change it."

You are not your business

As an entrepreneur, it's inevitable that apathy will creep in now and then. That's normal and it's nothing to panic about.

But when it lingers and days of apathy turn into weeks, it's usually not about the work at all. It's a signal. A quiet reminder that what you're doing might not be feeding you the way you thought it would.

Apathy is what happens when you chase the identity of "entrepreneur" without knowing who you really are. You think a successful business will fill the hole. That money, traction, or recognition will erase your doubt and finally make you feel complete. But those are sugar highs, not nourishment.

For a while, I thought being a ghostwriter and technical content marketer was an easy way to make money. It worked. I was good at it. It wasn't all that demanding. But then came the Trump tariffs, AI chaos, and economic instability. Then my complacency caught up with me, which slowed my business. Then I got lazy, deadlines slipped, and I assumed work would show up when I needed it.

In 2024, I actually lost money and lots of it. That snapped me out of it.

The work wasn't the issue. I lost my identity, confusing my business with my purpose. When business got tough, I had nothing else to stand on.

You are not your business. You are not your client roster, or your website, or your MRR. You're a human with a brain and a body and a set of beliefs. If you want to keep moving forward, you have to take care of that first.

Success won't fix your sense of self. But knowing who you are? That's the foundation everything else stands on.

Somewhere between life and death

Life and death are not binary states. You can be dead while still being very much "alive." (No, I'm not talking about being in a coma or vegetative state.) I call this state "not-dead."

You don't have to be Frankenstein's monster or a zombie to be "not-dead." You probably know several not-dead people. Perhaps you are not-dead yourself. I know I was not-dead in multiple periods of my life. Each day passes, nothing novel happens. Life stagnates and everything starts to suck.

Being not-dead is all about passive living. There's an Adam Sandler movie called Click where he can use a television remote control to fast-forward through boring parts of his life. It's essentially a re-telling of It's a Wonderful Life, but Sandler's character is much more not-dead than George Bailey. Click isn't a particularly good movie, but it does a good job of showing what a not-dead person lives like.

When I was in a not-dead state, I'd dread getting out of bed. I'd dread doing whatever I needed to do that day. I'd dread the end of the day because I hadn't made the most of the day. Dread dread dread. Not-dead.

Irenaeus once said, "The glory of God is man fully alive."

In that vein, **the glory of God is not man fully not-dead.**

Perpetual students never become masters

Need hardcore performance coaching? Look no further than Kapil Gupta. He is an absolutely brutal, no-nonsense truth-teller. His insights are often so frustratingly pointed, I sometimes feel embarrassed for myself while reading his books.

One of my favorite insights: "Perpetual students never become masters."

This is going to sound counterintuitive to many of you, but we need to **stop learning and start doing.** Even early on, entrepreneurs spend far too much time learning, prepping, and mitigating risk. It's laughable at times. There is no replacement for doing hard work and learning lessons "the hard way."

Nassim Taleb rightfully pointed out that the Wright Brothers didn't study how to make an airplane. They tinkered and built and the science of flight emerged afterwards. As I mentioned earlier, there is no science to business success, so there's no need to read read read all the literature.

Taleb calls people who do this "IYI" or "intellectual yet idiot" who "lecture birds on how to fly."

If you're not working on your business, you're either working in it or you're wasting time. Unless you're a 1-person business, you should not be spending all your time working as an employee. Your job is to build a sustainable, long-term future for yourself and your employees (if you have them).

Serious entrepreneurs aren't getting certifications, degrees, or more self-help books. They're making decisions, acting, and doing. You can't build a future sitting in the audience.

Preparation for letting go

Actually, honestly, and completely letting go of the mental prison bars is no easy thing. Seriously, when I first let go, I knew I was finally deciding to move on from decades of learned and addictive behavior. These were the questions running through my head at the time:

- Am I truly ready to let go of my mental prison? Do I actually want to do this?
- Is there a part of me that's resisting? If so, which part? Why is there resistance
- What's the worst that will happen if I let go of my mental prison bars today? Like, right now?
- What's the best that could happen if I let go?
- What will my life look like once I let go? Is this something I'm even able to understand or predict?
- If I let go, what can I do to resist the temptation to return? What would it look like to "burn the ships?"
- Do I want to live a better life? Do I want to believe in myself? Do I already believe in myself?

When I let go of my prison bars, my good friend, Markus Reuter, suggested I go look in the mirror and say, "You're perfect." He wasn't talking about actual perfection, but about being just as I am. The person who held the bars never needed the bars, but he may not be ready for living a life without them.

Only one way to find out.

READINESS: MAIN IDEAS

☞ Most entrepreneurs tolerate their mental prison until the pain of staying becomes unbearable.

☞ Letting go of limiting beliefs requires honest self-reflection.

☞ You have to want freedom more than familiarity. Otherwise, nothing changes.

☞ Being "ready" doesn't mean you won't be scared; it means you're willing to move anyway.

The opposite of a fact is falsehood, but the opposite of one profound truth may very well be another profound truth.

– Niels Bohr

Mental prison gut check

You don't need another podcast, book, or retreat. You don't need permission. You need to decide if you're actually ready to stop carrying the weight. Most of us say we want freedom, but when it shows up, we flinch. Dropping the bars takes more courage than picking them up. So ask yourself:

- What part of me is still benefitting from the prison?
- Who might I disappoint if I stopped playing small?
- What would I have to take responsibility for if I admitted I'm already free?
- What fear comes up when I imagine life without this weight?
- What would I do tomorrow if I stopped believing the worst things I think about myself?
- Am I afraid of being powerful?
- What identity would I lose if I stopped struggling?
- Do I really want freedom or just relief?
- What's more uncomfortable: staying stuck or finally moving forward?
- What does freedom look like to me, really?

Don't think of letting go of your mental prison bars as a grand gesture. It's really a quiet decision you'll make every day. It doesn't mean you're "healed" or have it all figured out. You're ready now not because the circumstances are perfect, but because you're done living behind bars you built yourself.

CHAPTER TWELVE

LETTING GO

There is nothing easier in the world than being yourself.

– Leonardo Pavkovic

Nothing easier in the world

This chapter started with a quote from my friend Leonardo Pavkovic: "There is nothing easier in the world than being yourself." Anything that stands in the way of being healthy and functional is a mental prison. When there is no mental prison, there is only a free individual.

Some people, like Leonardo, have never picked up the mental prison bars. They make no sense to him. For someone as unique and true to himself, picking up those bars would be like drinking arsenic to kick off the greatest day of his life.

Very few of us have it as "easy" as Leonardo, but Leonardo never saw difficulty in being himself. He is fortunate.

The rest of us want answers and security. Leonardo, on the other hand, wants to be himself. After all, who better to be Leonardo Pavkovic than Leonardo? We have every opportunity to simply be ourselves without giving it a second thought, but we have programmed ourselves to do otherwise.

He makes it look easy—because it is. There is nothing standing in the way of his will to be the most Leonardo Pavkovic that's ever existed.

One key lesson I learned playing some of the most challenging music ever written on guitar is: high performance is a side effect of effortlessness. Once I make a difficult task effortful, I've made it even more difficult.

So instead, I look to the Leonardos of the world and remind myself of how Anthony Garone would do it. Not the Anthony Garone who holds the mental prison bars, but the person he was intended to be with his once-in-a-universe DNA.

Relax, nothing is under control

Please don't look at this book as a "method" or a "framework," especially for "how to let go of your mental prison" or "how to succeed as an entrepreneur."

A method requires:

1. A set of path-dependent steps

2. Reproducibility

If you see a method in this book, it's because you want to. All I've done is organize information into collections of related information.

If there was something that "worked" for mental prisons, you would have heard about it by now. But there's no one-size-fits-all solution.

It's possible that prayer, meditation, walks, exercise, therapy, and a million other things could work, but chances are: they won't. Not that they can't. The issue is there is no "way" of doing it. You are looking for a prescription where there is none.

So, take a deep breath and relax. Nothing is under control.

What works and what doesn't

What did not get me out of my mental prison

- Knowledge
- Compliments and words of encouragement
- Time alone, time with friends and family
- Reading books (especially self-help)
- Work, career, hobbies
- Money, raises, bonuses
- New houses, cars, computers, guitars, gear
- Networking, meeting new people
- Food and/or alcohol, fancy restaurants
- Traveling, seeing new places
- Counselors and therapists
- TED Talks and inspirational speeches
- Online courses and tweet threads
- Podcasts, audiobooks, online courses
- Massages, working out, losing weight
- Winning awards, recognition, prizes
- Knowing celebrities and millionaires
- Serving the homeless, feeding the poor
- Meditative walks in nature
- Follower counts on social media

What did get me out of my mental prison

- Listening to Wisdom
- Deciding to change
- Sticking with the change every day

ACT like it's temporary

One of the most useful frameworks I've come across as an entrepreneur is Acceptance and Commitment Therapy (ACT). It helped me stop trying to eliminate fear, anxiety, and doubt. It also taught me to keep building with them in the room.

ACT, especially as described in The Mindfulness and Acceptance Workbook for Anxiety by Forsyth and Eifert, gave me a repeatable mental framework:

Accept what's showing up. Commit to what matters. Take action.

Before ACT, I used to think I needed to fix my mindset before launching something new. Or feel "ready" before making a hard call. But ACT flipped the order: the anxiety is the signal that something matters and the action is what frees you from the spiral. Not the other way around.

One exercise from the workbook helped me more than any other: a visualization of a rectangular room, floating in space. It has two doors, one on each end, and no ceiling. Picture it like a shoebox you can look down into. I imagine the difficult feeling or situation walking into the room. Maybe it's anxiety about losing a client. Or a specific person I dread emailing. I don't fight it, I don't fix it—I let it sit. Eventually, it walks through the other door. Always.

This practice taught me that feelings are temporary, even the big ones. Especially the big ones. And for business owners, that realization is powerful. It means I can do the hard, uncomfortable, or vulnerable thing, even while feeling overwhelmed. I don't need perfect clarity or calm to make good decisions. I just need to act.

I am separate from my thoughts

Another powerful technique I picked up from Acceptance and Commitment Therapy is called distancing language. It's simple, easy to practice, and surprisingly effective at breaking the spell of a mental prison.

Instead of thinking, "I'm not good enough,"

I say, **"I'm experiencing the feeling that I'm not good enough."**

Instead of, "I'm going to screw this up,"

I say, **"I'm noticing the fear that I might screw this up."**

It's a subtle shift, but it creates enough distance to remind myself that it's merely temptation to believe the negative thought. I'm no longer fused to my thoughts. Instead I'm observing them, naming them and giving them space between me and the them.

That space helps me to see that I am experiencing discomfort instead of being uncomfortable. Normally, when I say, "I'm hungry," I'm really saying, "I'm experiencing the feeling of hunger." But in the mental prison, when I say, "I'm an idiot," I rarely mean that I'm experiencing the feeling of being an idiot. I usually just jump into being an idiot.

As an entrepreneur, I've had days where I thought things like: I'll never run a successful business. I can't raise prices. I'll always work 12 hours a day. That voice can feel like the truth… until I apply distancing language and realize, Oh. That's fear talking again.

This practice doesn't erase the thoughts, but it does help them lose their grip.

I'm not my thoughts. I'm the one experiencing them.

Fight the system

Letting go of a mental prison can feel like an impossible ask because it is systemically hard. The "system" is the one between our ears and it is vicious. See this insightful post from Mark Baker, aka @GuruAnaerobic on X:

> Your beliefs have a type of 'immune system' which stops infiltration/infection from other ideas. The problem is this immune system can make you unable to progress; it attacks you - making you closed to new ideas.

When you've repeated negative beliefs for years ("I'm an idiot," "I'll never make this work," "I'm the worst entrepreneur ever") become deeply wired, to the point that they're automatic. Comfortable, even. The brain starts defending them, not questioning them. Any new belief, like the idea that "maybe I'm not an idiot," gets flagged as a threat.

That's why letting go of a mental prison can be so jarring. It's akin to overriding an immune system that sees progress as a virus. If you go to the gym and work hard, you can look in the mirror and see physical improvements. You can step on the scale and watch the number go down. But you can't easily measure whether that ol' brain of yours is rewiring old beliefs or just quietly rehearsing them in your subconscious mind.

So you soldier on without proof until you can look back and say, "Hey, things actually have gotten better. I haven't called myself an idiot in a few days."

Freedom doesn't come without a fight and letting go requires radical action.

There is only uncertainty. Yay!

Every day, entrepreneurs are trying to manage uncertainty and risk. We want to have a strong sense of control over our lives and businesses. This is foolish.

Uncertainty is not something to be feared or avoided. It's an inevitable (and joyful!) part of life and business. Yet most of us try to suppress it, to wrap ourselves in a cocoon of certainty and predictability. It's for this reason, a very small part of me gets irritated when someone wishes me "safe travels" or "stay safe." I'm not here to play it safe! I'm an entrepreneur! (I can hear you rolling your eyes.)

Uncertainty is where the real growth happens. It's where we're forced to confront our own limitations, to adapt to changing circumstances, and to innovate in response to new challenges.

So, let's flip this script. Let's stop trying to avoid uncertainty and start embracing it. Let's celebrate the fact that every day brings a new unknown, a new opportunity to learn, to grow, and to evolve.

This isn't to say that we should be reckless or impulsive. But rather, we should approach uncertainty with a sense of curiosity and wonder. We should be open to new ideas, new perspectives, and new experiences.

Get comfortable with not knowing what's next. Learn to love the unknown, to find joy in the uncertainty, and to trust that it will lead us to something better than we ever could have imagined.

It's entirely up to you

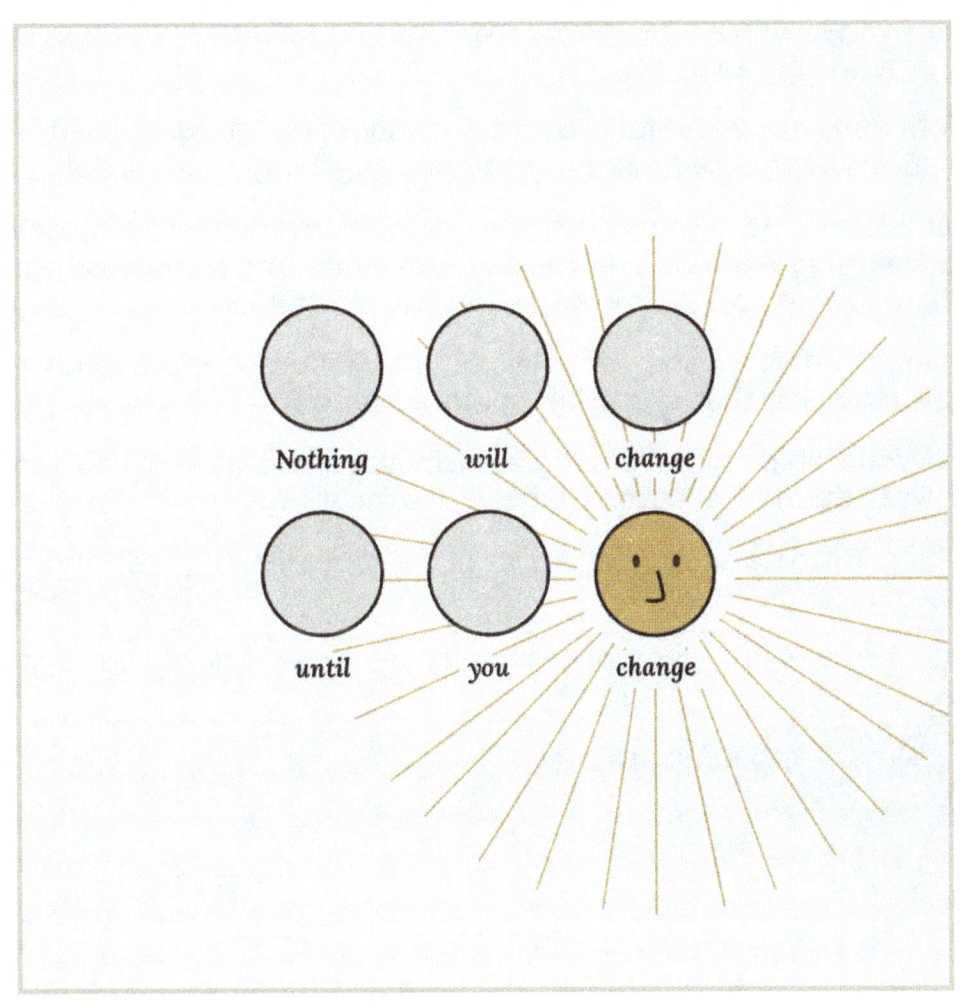

Used with permission. © Ash Lamb, ashlamb.com

So, play!

When you stop thinking everything is so dang important and has some deep meaning, you can kinda do whatever you want. As an entrepreneur, this can be as freeing as it is expensive.

There is right and wrong, but for most things there's no "good" or "bad." As Saint Paul once said, "Everything is permissible, but not everything is beneficial."

The bigger lesson here is to remove "meaning" from the task, project, effort, whatever. **Stop being so serious.** The moment I ascribe importance or meaning is the moment I am focused on the meaning, not the effort itself.

Focusing on the effort means I can play. I can try different approaches. I can engage that gut-level thinking that says, "This could work!"

Play is fun. Work can be play. Running a business can be like a game and you have to beat the competition. The reason it isn't: it has meaning.

Ugh, meaning. Nothing sucks the joy out of the room like purpose and meaning and significance.

Without it, it's play. With it, it's work. When I play, I'm effortless. I can experiment, enjoy, and react.

So, I play! It's much more fun anyway.

*Because children have abounding vitality, because they are in spirit fierce and free, therefore they want things repeated and unchanged.
They always say, "Do it again"; and the grown-up person does it again until he is nearly dead.
For grown-up people are not strong enough to exult in monotony. It is possible that
God says every morning, "Do it again" to the sun; and every evening, "Do it again" to the moon.
It may not be automatic necessity that makes all daisies alike; it may be that
God makes every daisy separately, but has never got tired of making them.
It may be that He has the eternal appetite of infancy; for we have sinned and grown old, and our Father is younger than we.*

– G.K. Chesterton, Orthodoxy

LETTING GO: MAIN IDEAS

☞ Letting go isn't a method. It's a decision that needs to be made daily.

☞ Effortlessness is the goal. Straining and overthinking are signs you're gripping too tightly.

☞ You don't have to be someone else to succeed. You just have to stop trying not to be yourself.

☞ Freedom is about accepting what is already here and choosing to respond.

Mental prison gut check

Letting go of the bars may not feel feel noble or graceful. In fact, it could be terrifying or even feel like failure. But for entrepreneurs, letting go is often the only way forward. We can't build something new while clinging to the beliefs, habits, or identities that held us back. Letting go is how we create space for better decisions, clearer thinking, and a business that isn't built around fear.

Ask yourself:

- What stories about myself am I still gripping like they're facts?
- Where do I keep reliving the past instead of building the future?
- Am I holding onto pain as a way to prove a point?
- What part of me wants to be wronged, misunderstood, or underestimated?
- Have I confused familiarity with truth?
- What would I have to feel if I let go of this grudge / identity / excuse?
- Who am I when I stop trying to prove I've been wronged?
- What has overstayed its welcome in my mind or business?
- Where am I seeking closure when I could simply move on?
- What's the real cost of hanging on?

Letting go requires activity. It's the opposite of giving up on your old ways, helping you to step into a position of power. When you drop what doesn't serve you, your hands are free to build something that does.

*Don't let people seduce you with the rhetoric of self-invention and being free to make up one's own values.
In the final analysis, there is no project duller and more suffocating than that.*

– Robert Barron

10 guiding principles and hard truths

1. **I'm not *in* prison.** I'm stuck in a negative thought loop that undermines my ability to run my business and make sound decisions.

2. **I'm not a thinking machine. I'm a feeling machine that thinks.** I rarely know what I'm going through until I've already gone through it. Only then do I create a story that makes sense in hindsight (and that story can change over time).

3. **I need to internalize positive feedback.** Compliments and hard truths don't fit inside a mental prison. If someone I trust says something good about me, I need to take it seriously.

4. **I control my company and my time.** No matter how tough the market is or how far success feels, I'm the one who decides what happens next.

5. **The devil wants me to fail.** He thrives in ambiguity, risk, and self-doubt. Don't let him in. And definitely don't eat his turd sandwiches, no matter who's serving them.

6. **I'm the maker of my own misery.** My thoughts, reactions, and emotions all originate with me. What happens to me isn't always my fault, but it is my responsibility.

7. **I can let go of the prison bars anytime.** No one is making me carry around guilt, shame, or fear. I can drop the bars. I just have to decide to.

8. **Freedom is uncomfortable, but it's better than the alternative.** I may have trained myself to live with doubt, stress, or fear, but I'm always more effective and happier outside the prison.

9. **I'm not alone.** There are thousands of entrepreneurs struggling with the same fears, doubts, and setbacks. Feeling alone isn't the same as being alone.

10. **There's no book, talk, or coach that can fix me.** No one else can live my life, run my business, or make my decisions. I'm the only one who can do the work.

PART TWO

Real-World Stories

Interviews with entrepreneurs who've let go of the bars.

My story: 30 years to stop believing myself and start believing in myself

You've certainly heard enough from me in this book, but you haven't actually heard a lot of my story. I don't remember when it started, but I clearly remember the first time I truly let go of the bars. In 2021, I was filming a music documentary across Europe when one day in Bosnia I heard a loud, clear voice in my head:

> **When will you stop ignoring the mountain of evidence that you are not a loser?**

Holding heavy a camera rig in my hand, I stopped for a moment and engaged as intelligently as I could with the voice. "Uh, what?"

The voice continued, "Who else do you know that's traveling across Europe on an all-expenses-paid trip with some of the world's greatest musicians? Who else is running their own business from across the ocean? Who else is spending entire days with his musical heroes, like Robert Fripp and members of Gentle Giant? Who else is married to a wonderful and successful woman with three healthy, intelligent children? **Is this the life of a loser?**"

The voice went on and on, asking me who else had a life as wonderful as mine. It was a constant barrage of authoritative, corrective questions for what felt like 10 minutes, but was probably an instant brain download. I heard the voice clear as day, but

MENTAL PRISONS

REAL-WORLD STORIES

knew it was in my own head. The camera continued recording as I walked backwards down the main thoroughfare of a town called Jajce.

After the voice stopped, I was on a manic high for months. Any notion of self-directed negativity was promptly smacked down as soon as it reared its head. There were a few instances where I almost reverted to old, self-deprecatory humor, but I immediately felt embarrassed at engaging with that part of myself. Instead, I felt warm inside, loved and cherished. It was incredible.

I truly felt like I was free of my mental prison. (Ha!)

Of course, nothing lasts forever, but I got a good 12-18 months out of the euphoric daily feelings of pure awesomeness. Writing this now in March 2025, I have an elevated awareness of when I regress to old, unhealthy behaviors. I'll be the first to admit, I could have handled my business circumstances much better since mid-2023 when my I felt business situation started to crumble. Bad decisions, overspending, and the disruption of AI took their toll. Thankfully I'm feeling like I'm back on the right track now.

But for about 30 years, I believed too much of my own internal BS. I like to say, **"I stopped believing myself and now I believe in myself."**

Now that I know what life is like after letting go of my bars, I operate with a few principles:

1. Stop thinking so much about myself, and when I do, be kind and humble.

2. When I fall into bad behaviors (and I know I will), get back up and try again.

3. Stick to the facts: The sky is blue and I have a wonderful life. Feelings are just data.

4. Failure is an opportunity to learn and change.

5. There is no hot without cold, there are no highs without lows.

6. I don't know what I'm going through until I've gone through it.

7. Remember the voice from Bosnia.

If it weren't for my business failures, music career stumbling blocks, and the fact that I cannot know everything about everything, I wouldn't be where I am today. Might I be somewhere better? Possibly. But, I'm reminded of a time I was talking to my friend Giovanni last year. I told him, "I always wanted to be a famous guitar player, but I gave that up a long time ago."

He replied, "Dude, you are a famous guitar player. You were in Guitar World Magazine. Steve Vai and Robert Fripp—two of your biggest music heroes—have talked about you publicly. You record music with some of the world's best musicians. Your YouTube channel has millions of views. What are you talking about?" I laughed and said, "Yeah, I guess you're right."

Yes, I've left a trail of dead LLCs behind me. On paper, they were legit attempts at making a business work, but looking back I can see that I wasn't dedicated enough or that I didn't allocate the energy they required.

I've also walked away from some big opportunities, like working for Steve Vai, Danny Hillis, and a couple of successful product teams. I quit those because I decided for other people that I wasn't good enough, smart enough, or worthy. As my kids would say, "Total beta behavior."

It's not that I didn't want to succeed. I just had so many misconceptions about the requirements. For instance, as a teenager, I (foolishly) thought the only requirement to being a rich and famous guitarist was being really good at guitar. Turns out that's not the case for nearly any industry. When I had to lean on skills I didn't know how to develop like charisma, marketing, sales, product market fit, I simply gave up.

I didn't believe I had what it'd take to make it and giving up is pretty easy. When I honestly reflect back on that time, I can see that I didn't have what it'd take, but my lack of self-belief made me believe it was impossible for me to achieve. And, honestly, it feels good to feel bad sometimes.

What I didn't understand back then was that **most entrepreneurs figure it out as they go.** I didn't know I could learn how to pitch, how to build a team, how to read a balance sheet, how to make good decisions under pressure. I assumed they were inherited traits and I didn't have the genetics.

So instead of learning them, I retreated. I stayed in my comfort zone and doubled down on what I was already good at, hoping that would be enough to carry me. It wasn't.

I look back now and don't feel shame. For the most part, I feel clarity and gratitude. Those missed opportunities, failed projects, and abandoned ideas were signs that I didn't believe I could accomplish my goals. Changing that belief is really what made the difference.

MENTAL PRISONS

Amy Looper

"I thought I just needed better time management."

Amy Looper didn't start her entrepreneurial career thinking she'd crash. For over 18 years, she crushed sales quotas, leading teams and climbing ladders. She built a strong reputation across multiple companies. Amy had what most entrepreneurs and execs chase: external success, recognition, momentum.

And then in 2020, she hit a wall.

After years of performing at a high level, burnout finally caught up. Her work was only one of the factors. She had faced postpartum depression after a traumatic birth. Her father-in-law had died by suicide. Her marriage was unraveling. Then she got fired from her high-paying executive role.

Like many achievers, Amy's first reaction wasn't so much grief as it was confusion. *"How come I can't keep going at this amazing upward pace?"*

The answer, she realized, had nothing to do with her inbox. She was living under a false set of beliefs that she was never "good enough." Childhood wounds had wired her for external validation. If people were happy, she was successful. If she hit the number, she was safe. Yet underneath it all, she felt like a fraud, chasing approval just to feel okay.

For the next two years, Amy worked incredibly hard on personal transformation. "I had to really look at how attached I was to external validation," she said. "I didn't realize how much I people-pleased. Or how much perfectionism was driving me. Or how much I was sabotaging myself by putting everyone else first."

Today, Amy coaches high-achieving women (especially working moms) who are caught in similar patterns. She seeks out women who want to lead, grow, parent, and thrive, but feel trapped by guilt, busyness, and the myth of "doing it all."

Her coaching goes deep. "We look at the root," she says. "We ask: where did this story come from? Who told you you had to prove yourself to be loved? What's it costing you to keep living that way?"

For Amy, faith became the foundation for breaking through. After trying to control everything for years, she had to give it up. "I did the self-help. I did the work. But the real freedom came when I gave up control to God. When I stopped forcing everything and started surrendering."

It might seem like Amy's fire went out, but it just got redirected.

She stopped asking, "How do I do more?" and started asking, "What do I want this life to actually feel like?"

Check out Amy's book, Leading Motherhood: Surrendering to Faith Over Fear From the Delivery Room to Board Room. You can learn more at amyleighlooper.com.

REAL-WORLD STORIES

Derek Walker

You won't get the time back and that's okay

Derek Walker spent 13 years at Pizza Hut before returning to his dream of working in advertising. Not because he lacked ambition, but because, like so many of us, he got caught in the rhythm of life: bills, responsibilities, routine.

He didn't realize he'd built a mental prison until a young driver at his store quit to take a job at Crispin Porter. That driver left behind a portfolio of ads that Derek brought home and showed to his pregnant wife. She flipped through the pages, looked at him, and said, "You're this good. When are you going?"

That was the turning point. He let go of the bars and walked out of his prison.

Later, his parents gave him another release: "You'll never catch up," they said. "You can't make up for lost time. You can only make the most of the time you have."

Derek went on to found his own agency, Brown & Browner, after years of agency work and a crash course in digital. But the dream only materialized when he let go of the need to "catch up" and focused on doing the work he knew he was here to do.

We all lose time. We all get trapped in the loop of living. The bars aren't always obvious. But when the moment to let go comes, you'll know.

And the next step is simple, even if it's not easy: Walk forward anyway.

Allen Plunkett
Hiring from insecurity

For years, Allen Plunkett hired salespeople based on a belief he didn't know he was carrying: *"Maybe they're not great because I'm not great."* He'd bring on aggressive closers with the stereotypical "sales guy" swagger because he didn't see himself as one. "I don't love selling," he said. "I've always felt like in this industry, you needed to be a real salesperson to be successful."

Instead of hiring based on the company's actual values (consultative, relationship-driven, down-to-earth) he was hiring to cover up a perceived personal shortcoming. That's where things started going sideways. "Not only did I not love their style, I didn't want my company to be seen that way." The mismatch led to internal friction, external discomfort, and lost business.

Allen recalled a former manager whose favorite sales analogy was: "You need to pull the arrow from your quiver, pin the client to the chair, and grab their wallet." It was that exact mentality he had tried to hire… until he couldn't stomach it anymore. Letting go of the last of those hires was one of the hardest terminations he's ever made. "It came as a surprise to him, which made me feel terrible. But it had to be done."

Looking back, he admits: "I didn't allow the thought to sit in my mind for too long. I just told myself, this is how it has to be. I have to do this to grow."

Once the decision was made, the shift was immediate. Clients who had remained quiet suddenly opened up: "That took too long," some said. They didn't like working with him either. "Now I tell my clients, if someone on my team isn't working for you, let me know. Don't wait."

The business didn't fall apart. In fact, it got much better. Best of all, Allen never hired a "sales guy" ever again.

Kurt Wilkin

You don't have to be good at everything

Kurt Wilkin spent years trying to be everything: founder, CPA, CEO, and more. He believed that meant mastering every corner of the business, whether or not he was any good at it. "Earlier in my career, I thought if I was the founder and we offered a service, I needed to be great at it," he said. "But the truth was: I wasn't. And pretending otherwise just made everything harder."

Many entrepreneurs fall for the belief that they need to do everything, or at least be capable of it all. For Kurt, that mindset came from watching his dad struggle to run a business solo. "He insisted on doing everything himself," Kurt recalled. "And he was as slow as Christmas."

Kurt brought that same "do-it-all" energy into his own company. Then reality caught up. Clients preferred his partners' technical work to his. Projects moved faster without him in the weeds. Most importantly, he realized his true gifts were elsewhere: building relationships, resolving difficult client conversations, and helping the business grow.

Still, letting go wasn't easy. "There was pride at stake," he admitted. "You feel lazy if you're not shoveling next to the team. But I had to ask myself: what's my highest and best use?" The answer wasn't spreadsheets or audit trails. It was being the person clients trusted when things went sideways.

Like the time a contractor on a big client project was caught surfing porn at work, then printing it out in black and white. "I showed up, owned it, fired the guy, refunded a bunch of money, and promised to make it right," Kurt said. "I had to be strong enough to stand up to the client while also supporting my team."

Today, Kurt helps other entrepreneurs recognize when they are the problem. "We all wear the mask of 'everything's fine,'" he said. "But the world doesn't want the mask. It wants the real you."

Barry Cleveland
Don't control the muse

I once told musician Barry Cleveland that fear of failure is a mental prison, especially for people who have already proven themselves. I've seen accomplished artists, entrepreneurs, and creators continue to doubt themselves even after years of success. It looks irrational from the outside.

Barry disagreed, but not in the way you might expect. He said, **"Maybe it's entirely rational to be aware of the contingency of creativity."** In other words: self-doubt isn't always dysfunction. Sometimes it's awareness not rooted in fear, but reverence.

"There's a denying principle that works against your sense of self," he told me. "That's not a bad thing. It might actually be what keeps you close to the source."

He explained it through a story about Mount Shasta, a 14,500-foot climb in Northern California. He attempted it once with a group that didn't take the preparation seriously. They barely made it up the mountain before they had to turn back.

A year later, one of the guys said he wanted a rematch with the mountain. Barry wasn't impressed.

"You've got the wrong attitude," he thought. "It's a mountain. You're just a little punk. If you're going to climb it, the right mindset is, 'Hello Mr. Mountain, please allow me to go to the top. Don't avalanche me. Don't kill me. By your grace, I'd like to visit your peak and come back down.' You're not beating the mountain."

The same, he said, applies to the muse.

Barry's made a career out of experimental, improvised music—most of it in collaboration with other world-class musicians. And still, after decades of practice, he doesn't claim to be in control of inspiration.

Yes, he has the craft. Yes, he can do solid work on command. But when the truly great moments happen and the music feels like it's coming from somewhere else entirely, it's about preparation and surrender.

He recalled an album he recorded with Richard Pinhas called Mu. They laid down the basic tracks in one afternoon. They never rehearsed together and never played together before. It was pure improvisation. No edits. One 30-minute piece of music, created in real time. Barry said, "That was lucky. You can spend hours trying to capture something like that and get nothing. That was lightning."

Another example is his band Cloud Chamber. They had no setlists or structure. They walked on stage to see what'd happen. That kind of gig is a tough sell. What club wants to hear, "We don't have material, but trust us"? But they kept doing it because they had two things: craft, and the belief that the muse might show up.

Sometimes it did. Sometimes it didn't. But it showed up often enough that they trusted it. It wasn't because they were sure, but because they had learned to create the right conditions for it to happen.

"There's a level of skill, and then there's something greater," Barry told me. "When I'm working here at home, I know I can write something solid. That's craft. But what I'm hoping for—that thing that makes the audience go 'What just happened?'—that's not up to me."

He described it like a ritual. You prepare yourself, create the space, do your incantations, and then you wait in humility.

If you've done something extraordinary before, and you keep showing up with the same care and intention, it will probably happen again. Not every time. But enough times to keep going. **There is strength in respecting the process.**

Brad Lemley

"The only way out is through"

Brad Lemley is a former science journalist for *Discover Magazine* and the *Washington Post*. On his website, he shares a compelling story about pushing through his own "debilitating panic attacks in one hour." It's available as a free download. Here's the short version.

Brad was "nearly afraid of everything" since he was a child. His biggest fear was revealing his fearfulness to the world, but like me, he combatted it with his intellect. As he found success in his growing career, the anxiety grew, so he ended up moving to rural Maine to escape everyday life. This move made him lonelier and more terrified than ever, which led to seizure-like collapses in his hallway. He screamed and convulsed until he fully passed out.

After several of these bouts, he had a new, inexplicable idea: have the next panic attack in front of as many people as possible. He would drive his car to a crowded space and scream publicly. So, he did. He went to the store, worked himself up, and… couldn't cause the panic attack.

He hasn't had a panic attack since then. It's been almost 30 years.

While I've never been inclined to go out in public and broadcast my insecurities (that's what this book is for), I understand what happened. When I feel a challenge coming on, I go straight into it. The shortest route between two points is a straight line. No sense in beating around the bush, circuitously avoiding a problem.

Don't delay and don't resist. Go into the problem head-first and show it who's boss.

Chris Opperman
The meritocracy myth of academia

Chris Opperman spent over a decade chasing a single goal: a full-time tenure-track role in academia. He had the qualifications. He had the experience. He had the drive. He believed that if he simply outperformed everyone, he'd eventually land the job. A little studying, a little memorization, and some pedagogical elbow grease and he'd be in charge. Probably.

"I thought by outperforming everybody that that would be key," he said. "But I had professors literally sit and tell me, 'This is not a meritocracy. If it was, you'd be running the school.'"

He didn't believe them, so he ignored them. For 11 years.

He believed so strongly in what the job represented (stability, purpose, recognition) that he tolerated politics, poor leadership, and even public disrespect. "I really wanted it bad," he admitted. "Getting a tenured professorship was literally the difference between being rich and not being rich."

When the job finally went to someone clearly unqualified ("The guy walked into the interview and had the students coloring"), it shattered what was left of the illusion. A department chair had promised him a promotion if he stayed on through the pandemic. Then he denied it ever happened. "He told me I was imagining a promise he never made, so I packed up my suitcase and walked out."

Quitting was both an act of self-respect and a turning point. He shifted all the energy he'd been giving away back into his own ambitions. He started a business that now earns more each month than he used to make in a year. Instead of waiting for validation and chasing a broken system, he let go of the bars.

In doing so, he found what he was after all along: impact, independence, and proof that his value never needed permission.

Kara Hughes
Brain cancer, stroke, a heart attack, and still going

Kara was born deaf. She taught herself to hear. Her mother was autistic and struggled to show affection, so Kara learned emotional connection by necessity, not inheritance. And that was just the start.

In her 30s, Kara became a single mom and then got the kind of diagnosis that stops time: brain cancer. "Best 35th birthday gift, amirite?" she joked.

But she didn't collapse under the weight of it. She told herself, "Nope. Not today. This is going in the rearview."

Over the next decade, Kara lived through a stroke, heart failure, and a heart attack. That would break most people. But not Kara. She kept going, raising her daughter, working in tech, paying bills, showing up.

"I don't like the word 'challenges,'" she told me. "I don't think of my life that way."

She talked about walking to school as a kindergartener, unable to hear traffic, alert to every movement in the world. "I've walked through life with my eyes open ever since."

Her approach to survival? Not fight. Not denial. Curiosity.

"When you get brain cancer, you realize: you can live without a foot, but you can't live without a brain. So when they gave me that diagnosis, I thought, 'Okay. This is it. Nothing will touch me after this.'" She didn't mean it in a defiant way. She meant it like someone who had seen the very worst and still chose to breathe.

Kara believes our bodies speak for us when we can't. "I don't want people to hear this and think I'm saying, 'You're to blame for your illness,'" she said. "But we all carry pain. We all have energy stuck in us. Stories we've never examined. That stuff doesn't just live in your brain. It lives in your cells."

She sees health as a reflection of what we've yet to face. She encourages people to ask: Where am I holding pain that never got a voice?

Only one person ever called her "sick." She did not like that. **"What part of me is sick?"** she asked. **"Because I go to the doctor? Because my heart needed help? That's not who I am."**

She views everything as energy. "Your temple is within. If you don't look inward, how can you ever understand what's stuck there? You have to ask: What is this diagnosis here to teach me? What do I need to move? And if that sounds mystical, just remember: it's not about being right. It's about being present."

While battling cancer and raising her daughter, Kara started a nonprofit. Then a second one. Then a third.

She launched a holiday support program for single moms with cancer, collecting donated gifts and delivering them to families who'd otherwise go without. She started a refurbished phone and laptop program so moms could stay connected. She worked with artists to hand-paint medical helmets and braces for kids, turning them into tiny superheroes.

She calls her latest effort Relentless Spirit—a spiritual mentorship rooted in faith and spoken word. "God calls the messages to my heart," she said. "I share what I hear."

Her faith keeps her grounded. Her daughter keeps her moving. Her joy keeps her open.

"You can't always be taught how to find your strength," she said. "But it's there. You just have to access it."

Then she paused.

"When you feel overwhelmed, breathe deep into your gut. Look around. Smell the air. Hear the world. Find three things you're grateful for. The monkey brain wants to take over. But you have the power to bring yourself back."

And Kara would know. She's come back from everything.

Patricia Fripp

Work ethic, wisdom, and working through fear

Patricia Fripp grew up thinking she wasn't as smart as the people around her. Her brother Robert was "the genius" (yes, that Robert Fripp), and she frequently thought, "Well, I'm probably not as smart as my brother or the other kids in my class." It was a belief that stuck with her through school and her early career.

Fripp didn't fight her mental prison with self-help books or a bolt of lightning. She fought it with repetition, hard work, and relentless follow-through. When the other hairstylists did two models, she did five. When they took lunch, she squeezed in four more clients. Consistency, not comparison, became her foundation.

That mindset paid off. At 19, she was told she brought in 30% more revenue than the "superstars" around her. When others in her industry questioned her success, she had a simple reply: "Why should anyone resent my success? I worked six and a half days a week and long hours."

Eventually, she left hair behind and quickly rose to become the first female president of the National Speakers Association. Not because she asked to, but because someone saw her potential. And when opportunity knocked, she didn't let impostor syndrome take over.

This led her to one thing she feared most: running board meetings. For eight months, she listened to cassette tapes on parliamentary procedure for hours at a time. When she finally led her first board meeting, one of the most respected members of the organization told her, "I've never seen anyone show more expertise and knowledge about parliamentary procedure than you."

Fripp's transformation didn't come from feeling ready. She studied hard, practiced, and executed with authority. Over time, she rewrote the story: from "I'm not smart" to "I'm capable, prepared, and more consistent than anyone else in the room."

Learn more about Patricia and get her expert advice at fripp.com.

REAL-WORLD STORIES

Phillip Oakley

Other people's beliefs helped me lay down the bars

When Phillip Oakley started the renowned marketing agency, Common Giant, he set out to do good work and stay creative. But along the way, he hit a familiar wall: the belief that he wasn't good enough.

"I can't tell you how many times I've thought, 'We don't offer that service' or 'I don't know that' and then realized: Wait… I can learn anything," he said. But like many entrepreneurs and creatives, Phillip often defaulted to self-doubt. "You get started, and it's shit. Then you think: I'm shit. And it's hard to break out of that cycle."

He found the courage to push through, not because of some magical self-realization event, but because others believed in him when he didn't. It started early, when he was unexpectedly voted captain of his high school varsity soccer team. "It wasn't my skillset, but all the other things I brought, and I had no idea people saw that in me."

That pattern repeated throughout his life. "Friends, clients, teammates—so many people told me I was doing great work and I just couldn't see it," he said. "It was easier to believe they were being polite than to believe I was actually that good."

The moment that stuck most came during a rough stretch. He hadn't paid himself in months, was considering selling his car, and felt like he was dragging his team down. Then, a former client and friend reached out just to say: "People read what you write. You're one of the only thought leaders who actually has something to say."

That shook something loose. "It helped me get through the 'I'm shit' phase," Phillip said. "And made me realize: the real gold is just on the other side of that wall."

He still wrestles with bars (fear of losing clients, impostor syndrome, ego) but now he can see them. "Sometimes you're so used to the bars that when someone tries to hand you new ones, you happily accept them. You don't even question it." But he's learning that every time someone believes in him, it gets a little easier to believe in himself.

Steve Mueller
From engineer to CEO and software startup founder

One of Steve's earliest limiting beliefs was that he wasn't CEO material. "I thought I'd be a lifelong technologist," he said. "I didn't know cap tables or how to raise money. I didn't think I could learn that stuff." He viewed himself as the "in-house foster kid," not the founder of his own company.

But when a million-dollar lawsuit landed on his desk, that self-image had to go. He led his company through the challenge, and more importantly, he learned to see himself differently. He was much more than a builder.

There was another, deeper prison too: believing he didn't need anyone else. He'd always operated solo, fueled by talent, drive, and a chip on his shoulder. "I thought I didn't need friends, didn't need partners. Just intelligence and hard work." But starting a company made that belief impossible to hold on to. He had to let people in, build trust, and let go of the lone-wolf mindset.

Today, Steve runs a venture-backed company and openly talks about the recurring nature of mental prisons. "You never fully escape them," he said. "They just change shape." Some days it's impostor syndrome. Other days, it's fear of being seen as weak. Or the creeping belief that I'm not leading 'well enough.'" His hardest lessons:

- Push the button and take the first step. Action leads to clarity. Waiting for the "right time" is often a way to stay stuck. Having a bias toward action beats overthinking.
- Impostor syndrome doesn't go away. But you can learn to notice it, challenge it, and keep going anyway.
- The beliefs you have about yourself become business policies. If you don't believe in your value, others won't either and they'll behave accordingly.

Ali Schwanke
Misunderstood ≠ Broken

Ali Schwanke always saw patterns before others did. Whether it was a market shift, a customer behavior trend, or an inefficiency in a process, she had a knack for connecting dots others couldn't see. Unfortunately, her foresight came at a price. Early in her career, when leaders didn't act on her insights, she internalized the response: *Maybe I'm not as smart as I think I am.* It was a turd sandwich that she "needed to work harder, prove more, and know everything before speaking up."

She didn't lack intelligence or discipline. Ali was already running circles around peers with her output and strategic thinking. The real trap was her belief that if people didn't get her, it meant she was the problem. Over time, that mental loop turned into a pattern of over-compensating. Every time her gut said "this is the direction," and others pushed back, she'd double down on research and proof till she was exhausted.

Then she started working with a therapist who understood high-performing entrepreneurs. Instead of trying to "fix" her, the therapist helped her build an "evidence chart" with a record of past gut decisions, what she saw early, and how things played out. She finally had proof of having insights years ahead of their time, giving her newfound confidence.

That shift helped her build boundaries around where she spent her energy. "Maybe I'm just in the wrong room," she realized. Rather than convincing people who couldn't see the opportunity, she began choosing clients who valued foresight and strategy. What had once felt like a curse turned into a filter. If someone didn't "get it," maybe they weren't meant to.

Her prison didn't vanish. The voice still tries to creep in: "You need to know more. You need to make them see it." But Ali now knows what that voice sounds like and how to push back. Misunderstanding no longer signals personal failure. It's just a reminder that being early is lonely, and sometimes the only way forward is to change the room, not yourself.

Lisl Macdonald
The illusion of upward momentum

At a young age, Lisl Macdonald flew up the corporate ladder: head of strategy, then a global C-suite role, all before she hit 30. The titles were shiny. The budgets were big. The trajectory was relentlessly onward and upward. But something felt wrong. "I didn't actually want it," she admits. "I enjoyed the intellectual challenge, but not the politics, the pace, or the pressure." When a political reshuffling ended her tenure, it turned out to be the best gift she never asked for.

Rather than chasing another executive title, she went the opposite direction—literally. She traveled around the world alone, pre-smartphone, exploring remote villages in Laos, India, Kenya, and Indonesia. "I realized I wasn't tethered to anything," she says. "I wanted a life that was fascinating, not impressive." That realization broke a lifelong mental pattern: the belief that success only came through sanctioned authority and corporate progression. Instead of another job title, she sought freedom.

She settled in Southeast Asia and took up university lecturing while picking up side consulting projects. But when a client asked her to form a company and offered a retainer, something clicked. "I guess I needed someone else to give me permission," she says. She set up her own firm in Thailand and started hiring collaborators for larger projects. "I wasn't freelancing anymore. I was building something."

Today, Lisl's life revolves around flexibility and fulfillment. She works when there's work, sails when there isn't, and surrounds herself with collaborators she respects. She still battles the occasional whisper of old mental prisons, like what others think, or what her résumé says. But those voices don't drive her anymore. "Freedom is the goal," she says. "Not just financial, but creative, personal, emotional."

For Lisl, the badge of honor isn't a job title, but the ability to own your time, choose your clients, and walk away from toxic situations. "In Asia, being a business owner means something, even if it's just a coffee cart," she says. "There's admiration for grit, not just status. That's the kind of recognition that actually matters."

REAL-WORLD STORIES

Ken Bogard
Obsessed with Perfection

Ken Bogard started his business consultancy in his mid-thirties with a familiar fear: I'm too young. Who's going to take me seriously? That turd sandwich was fed to him by someone else, and it stuck. Leading strategic sessions for CEOs and executives twice his age, Ken felt he had to overcompensate. It wasn't enough to know the material. He had to be perfect. "I became obsessed with polish and performance," he recalls. "It wasn't healthy, but it worked—at first."

As he earned clients and confidence, the age-based fear faded. Then something more subtle replaced it: the belief that success meant control. He noticed his strategy teams struggling because they lacked honesty. "They couldn't tell each other the truth," Ken said. "They weren't lying, but they were afraid of consequences, of judgment, of each other." This realization birthed No Honesty, his book about how openness and honesty transform teams, families, and lives.

But even writing No Honesty came with its own trap. Ken spent months hiring ghostwriters, rejecting drafts that didn't capture his voice. The perfect collaborator was beside him the whole time: his assistant, Grace Gavin. Brilliant, intuitive, and two decades younger, she stepped in and co-wrote the book. And still, Ken hesitated. "I wanted to take all the credit," he admits. "It was selfish, fear-based, and small." Eventually, he chose to share authorship and watched Grace rise in her own career. That shift from ego to partnership was a breakthrough.

Ken now sees mental prisons not as one-time events, but recurring patterns. "You escape one, and then a new one sneaks in," he says. "But I catch them quicker now, before the bars go up." His work helping others speak freely has shaped his own growth, too. He's more patient, generous, and aware. "I care less about being perfect and more about being clear and kind."

The book he once wanted all to himself is now a shared success. The career he feared he was too young to build became his calling. And the mindset that once obsessed over control now centers on curiosity, compassion, and contribution. As Ken says, "Mental prisons don't go away. But you can stop decorating the cell."

REAL-WORLD STORIES

MENTAL PRISONS

I will not be pushed, filed, stamped, indexed, briefed, debriefed, or numbered. My life is my own.

– Number Six, The Prisoner

Are we ever free?

Letting go of a mental prison can feel like an impossible ask because it is systemically hard. The "system" is the one between our ears and it is vicious. See this insightful post from Mark Baker, aka @GuruAnaerobic on X:

> *Your beliefs have a type of 'immune system' which stops infiltration/infection from other ideas. The problem is this immune system can make you unable to progress; it attacks you - making you closed to new ideas.*

When you've repeated negative beliefs for years ("I'm an idiot," "I'll never make this work," "I'm the worst entrepreneur ever") become deeply wired, to the point that they're automatic. Comfortable, even. The brain starts defending them, not questioning them. Any new belief, like the idea that "maybe I'm not an idiot," gets flagged as a threat.

That's why letting go of a mental prison can be so jarring. It's akin to overriding an immune system that sees progress as a virus. If you go to the gym and work hard, you can look in the mirror and see physical improvements. You can step on the scale and watch the number go down. But you can't easily measure whether that ol' brain of yours is rewiring old beliefs or just quietly rehearsing them in your subconscious mind.

So you soldier on without proof until you can look back and say, "Hey, things actually have gotten better. I haven't called myself an idiot in a few days."

Freedom doesn't come without a fight and letting go requires radical action.

Not everyone wants freedom

Of course, we have to acknowledge the reality that not everyone actually wants to be free. The mental prison is far too comfortable and safe to truly want to escape.

Some people love their mental prison. It gives them an identity. It gives them someone to blame. It gives them an excuse to play small, stay comfortable, and avoid the hard work of freedom. The prison lets them say, "This is just how I am."

They've grown attached to the suffering, the story, and the feeling of being the underdog, the misunderstood genius, the one who "could've" if only the world had been fair.

Freedom requires responsibility. It means owning your mistakes, admitting when you've been wrong, and doing things that scare the hell out of you. Freedom means letting go of the story you've been telling yourself and writing a new one without knowing how it ends.

Not everyone is ready for that. I know I wasn't, and in many ways, I'm still not ready.

And that's fine. But if you're still reading this book, you might be ready to change. You've felt the weight of the bars. You know the prison isn't real. And you're starting to see that the only thing keeping you stuck is you.

Freedom might feel awkward at first. Unfamiliar. Lonely, even.

But it's better than pretending you're locked up when the door's been open the whole time. In fact, the door never really existed in the first place.

The one worthwhile idea in this book

It's not clear to me how much of this book is True, but if there's one thing I've learned exploring this topic it's this:

We have exactly the life (and business) we want.

We are the architects of the bars and our freedom.

This belief, which comes to me from Kapil Gupta, has become a lens I use daily. Almost everything I complain about is something I've said yes to. And when friends call to vent about their own lives, I rarely hear a story that couldn't have been avoided, or at least responded to differently.

When I say I'm "too busy," it's because I said yes to too many things.

When I feel isolated, it's because I didn't reach out to anyone.

When I feel stuck, it's because I haven't chosen a way forward.

As an entrepreneur:
I signed the contracts that burned me out.
I negotiated the bad deals.
I made the wrong hires.
I didn't act when the red flags started waving.

I may not have "wanted" these outcomes, but I wanted something about them badly enough to let them happen and continue happening. If I can escape a situation, I must have helped build it.

The only real mental prison is believing I had nothing to do with where I am.

The only real freedom is realizing I have far more control than I ever let myself believe.

OTHER BOOKS BY ANTHONY GARONE:

CLUELESS AT THE WORK (2019)
FAILURE TO FRACTURE (2021)
WINNING THE JOB SEARCH (2022)

All books published by Stairway Press,
an independent book publisher based in Apache Junction, Arizona

THANKS FOR READING.

Please leave a review on Amazon, Goodreads, and your favorite social media network.
Please use #mentalprisons

LinkedIn: @anthonygarone
Twitter: @atgarone
Facebook: @anthony.garone
TikTok: @anthonygarone

My Amazon page: https://www.amazon.com/author/anthonygarone
Goodreads: https://www.goodreads.com/anthonygarone

THANKS FOR READING.

ANTHONY GARONE

"Thinking in isolation and with pride ends in being an idiot." – G.K. Chesterton

www.ingramcontent.com/pod-product-compliance
Lightning Source LLC
Chambersburg PA
CBHW081024240426
43671CB00029B/2926